Reflective Analysis
of Student Work

This book is dedicated to my loving mother,
June, and beloved father, Mike, for teaching me the
most valuable lessons in life and giving of
themselves so that I could achieve my dreams.

Reflective Analysis *of* Student Work

Improving Teaching Through Collaboration

Norene J. Bella

CORWIN PRESS
A Sage Publications Company
Thousand Oaks, California

For information:

Corwin Press
A Sage Publications Company
2455 Teller Road
Thousand Oaks, California 91320
www.corwinpress.com

Sage Publications Ltd.
6, Bonhill Street
London EC2A 4PU
United Kingdom

Sage Publications India Pvt. Ltd.
B-42, Panchsheel Enclave
Post Box 4109
New Delhi 110 017 India

Printed in the United States of America

Library of Congress Cataloging-in-Publication Data

Bella, Norene J.
Reflective analysis of student work : improving teaching through collaboration / by Norene J. Bella.
    p. cm.
Includes bibliographical references (p.   ) and index.
ISBN 0-7619-4597-0—ISBN 0-7619-4598-9 (pbk.) 1. Group work in education.
2. Reflective teaching. 3. Effective teaching. I. Title.
LB1032.B44 2004
371.39′5—dc22

                                                                2003021394

This book is printed on acid-free paper.

03   04   05   06   07   08   10   9   8   7   6   5   4   3   2   1

Acquisitions Editor:	Rachel Livsey
Editorial Assistant:	Phyllis Cappello
Production Editor:	Julia Parnell
Copy Editor:	Diana Breti
Proofreader:	Taryn Bigelow
Typesetter:	C&M Digitals (P) Ltd.
Indexer:	Sylvia Coates
Cover Designer:	Tracy E. Miller
Graphic Designer:	Anthony Paular

Contents

Preface

If we accept that the industrial model of society is currently shifting to a learning model of society, then the focus of education must also shift. The change will require a movement away from a content-driven curriculum toward a curriculum that provides individuals with the skills necessary to engage in lifelong learning.

Simultaneously, the role of the educator needs to shift from the information provider to that of a catalyst, coach, innovator, researcher, and collaborator with the learner throughout the learning process. The development of the learner's unique abilities becomes the central focus of the learning environment.

—Costa & Liebmann, 1997a, p. xxi

WHY THIS BOOK AND WHY NOW?

The shifts in the focus of education and the role of educators that Costa and Liebmann have spent years researching and writing about present an enormous challenge for educators today. They require that teachers, school administrators, professional developers, curriculum directors, and mentors think outside the educational box they have become so comfortable with.

Today's society demands that these shifts in thinking take place so that all students can obtain the skills and attitudes necessary to be productive and contributing citizens. Students must have solid content knowledge. They must acquire essential understanding of fundamental concepts and exhibit their understanding in a variety of circumstances. At the same time, students must know how to begin and what processes to use when they are faced with new situations beyond the context of the classroom. However, to successfully accomplish this, schools must be committed to helping educators shift the focus in all areas of their practices. Educators need to shift from teaching isolated content to teaching content in a way that promotes the development of essential thinking skills and processes. It requires a shift from textbook-driven curriculum to an emphasis on learning through real-life problem solving experiences. These experiences must encourage the students to constantly question and seek answers, constructing and refining their knowledge base as they proceed. To support this type of process-oriented learning, teachers need to create classrooms in which interaction between students, and between students and teacher, is valued. They must create classrooms in which teachers and students collaborate, and the role of the teacher shifts from that of the leader on stage to that of expert, facilitator, and co-learner working with students to form cooperative problem-solving teams. In these classrooms, the skills of a lifelong learner are being modeled by the teachers and nurtured in every student.

To state that these shifts in education will be an enormous task would be stating it lightly. But they are shifts that are vital to the students of today who will be our leaders of tomorrow. Many teachers have started to make these vital shifts in their practices and are encouraged by the excitement and commitment of their students. Many institutes of higher education, educational service centers, and other educational initiatives are currently taking a closer look at these teachers and their practices.

During the time that I worked on one such project, it was evident that truly committed professionals are starting to make these vital shifts. In addition, the belief that truly committed professionals continually evaluate themselves was validated in discussions with teachers and administrators from seventeen school districts throughout Ohio. Countless discussions with exemplary teachers also confirmed that teachers believe in the power of collaboration so deeply that they will find the time in their busy schedules for these dialogues. Interviews with numerous administrators revealed that they too saw the value in collegial discussions centered on teaching and learning, and they also realized the tremendous impact these discussions have on a teacher's practice. Visits to schools and conversations with students from elementary through high school had the recurring theme that students feel they learn best when their teachers nurture and construct a process-oriented learning environment for them. Working on this project was a powerful experience for me, during which I attended and presented at conferences throughout the United States to gather further insights and to continue the dialogue with educators, administrators, and students outside Ohio. As well, I held workshops with teachers in Ohio to discuss student work and to record the effects these conversations had on the teachers' practices.

As I reentered the teaching profession after a year and a half, I realized how deeply my views on teacher practice had been affected. I found myself looking differently at everything I did in my own classroom, at the work students were doing throughout my elementary building, and at the entire school system. I became increasingly interested in the unit design work of Wiggins and McTighe (1998), the research of Costa and Liebmann (1997a) into indicators of intelligent behavior, and Schlechty's (1997) research on effective Design Qualities of student work. At the same time, I was mentoring teachers who were completing the National Board for Professional Teaching Standards Certification process, having become a National Board Certified Teacher myself several years earlier. As I mentored these teachers, and discussed with them the work they had created for their students and were putting into their professional teaching portfolios, I came to realize that possibly the most powerful form of professional development occurs when teachers discuss student work and then, through reflection, use what they learned to direct their professional development endeavors and strengthen their practices. Not only did I feel it was extremely important to make vital shifts in education today, I felt it was extremely important to make it clear how these shifts could be accomplished in every classroom headed by a truly devoted teacher. From firsthand experience, I knew how hard it was to incorporate current research and educational initiatives into a teacher's practice. With the increasing demands imposed on every teacher, there is little time to restructure our practices and incorporate even the most powerful research that we read about or experience through workshops and higher education classes. As a result, a comprehensive Collaborative Professional Development Process evolved that combines elements of the research of Costa and Liebmann and Schlechty with firsthand teaching experience.

In Chapter 1, Figure 1.1 illustrates how research and everyday teaching experience can blend together into a powerful collaborative professional development initiative—an initiative that begins with teachers self-evaluating, and then in collaboration with trusted colleagues evaluating their practices through structured analysis of the work they design for their students. The Collaborative Professional Development Process relies heavily on the reflective skills of every educator to take what they learn about their practices in the collaborative discussion sessions and use it to design their personal Professional Development Plans.

A DIFFERENT APPROACH TO PROFESSIONAL DEVELOPMENT

This book is different because it not only puts teachers in charge of their own professional development, it does so through a highly reflective framework that uses the everyday work their students produce. It is through student work, and in collaboration with their colleagues, that teachers analyze their practices and determine the areas that need improvement to make their teaching and their students' learning as meaningful as possible. Many initiatives are being developed today that look at student work. Standards in Practice developed by The Education Trust, the Collaborative Assessment Conference developed by Harvard's Project Zero, and the Tuning Protocol developed by the Coalition of Essential Schools are only a few of these initiatives. This collaborative professional development initiative is unique in that there is no head facilitator or leader for the collaborative discussions of student work. Instead, every educator who is part of a collaborative team is equal to all the other members. The carefully designed guide for the collaborative discussions of student work is structured in such a way that every member of the team contributes and facilitates, but no one rules. This eliminates the fear of judgment by one's peers and puts all the participants on the same level, making the process truly collaborative in nature. The incorporation of Schlechty's (1997) Design Qualities and Costa and Liebmann's (1997a) Intellectual Engagement Indicators into the discussions of student work also makes this particular approach unique. The Collaborative Professional Development Process not only focuses the discussions of student work on sound research, it gives the presenting teachers this same research base as a framework on which to build their Professional Development Plans.

ORGANIZATION AND CONTENTS

This book is organized around two central themes. It is conceptual, in that it brings together the research of Costa, Liebmann, and Schlechty, and blends it with the research conducted in schools throughout Ohio. It outlines a collaborative professional development framework that puts educators in charge of their own professional development through reflective and collaborative practices. It ensures that these professional development endeavors are aimed at making the vital shifts in education that are needed to prepare every student to become a productive, contributing member of society and a lifelong learner. This book is also developmental, in that it provides educators with the professional learning activities that are needed to guide their professional development and teaching practices.

Chapter 1 is an overview of the Collaborative Professional Development Process. The process begins with the formation of collaborative learning teams. Educators work with trusted colleagues to examine student work. Through reflection, teachers determine whether their professional development goals have been met and define new professional development goals to pursue.

Chapter 2 describes the professional standards that form the foundation of the Collaborative Professional Development Process. It also introduces the Intellectual Engagement Indicators developed by Costa and Liebmann and the Design Qualities developed by Schlechty.

Chapter 3 addresses the need for reflection in every teacher's practice and provides suggestions for becoming more reflective in all aspects of one's practice. The role that reflective practices play in the Collaborative Professional Development Process is addressed throughout this chapter.

Chapters 4 and 5 are devoted to an in-depth explanation of Guided Collaborative Discussion of Student Work. Included in the chapters are worksheets to help educators complete the process.

Chapter 6 addresses the development of the highly personal Professional Development Plan, based on the teacher's reflections during the first four steps of the process. It goes on to explain how subsequent collaborative discussions of student work are used to gather evidence of teachers' growth in their professional development focus areas.

Chapter 7 explains how to design quality lessons and includes sample plans and blank unit design worksheets.

Chapter 8 explores instructional strategies, with a focus on the changing role of the teacher.

Chapter 9 explains the importance of analyzing lessons during implementation and includes worksheets to use while carrying out the recommended strategies.

Finally, in the Resource section is a sample school calendar that incorporates all the key elements into a schedule that begins the first month of the school year. Educators will find that it will help them to begin thinking about using the Collaborative Professional Development Process to guide their professional lives and help their students to become lifelong learners ready to function in the "real world."

Acknowledgments

Foremost I would like to acknowledge my caring mother, sisters, and their families for their unconditional love and support during the writing of this book. Without their constant loving force in my life, this book would never have been written while I carried on a full-time career in my classroom. They came through for me in countless ways when the completion of this book seemed so far away. Their love is my guiding focus and I will be forever grateful to them.

To my fun-loving nephew, Robbie. Thank you for your belief in me and adoration of my teaching that has always made me strive to reach higher. You are an amazing young man with a keen gift for recognizing the quality educators in your own life. Your insights, loving heart, and passion for life inspire me daily and will make your life a wonderful, rewarding adventure. I love you like a son.

To my "princess" niece, Mylane. Thank you for your endless supply of kisses and hugs that make me feel like the luckiest aunt in the world. You have such a brilliant young mind and loving heart. I know you will do great things some day. You are my precious little angel.

To my wonderful sister Karla and brother-in-law Rob. Thank you for your support and love that have seen me through so much and for which I will be forever grateful. I admire and love your commitment to our family.

To my caring niece Dawnya and her husband Michael. Thank you for all your technical support and computer expertise as I wrote this book. Your compassion for others and willingness to help touches my heart.

I'd especially like to recognize Rachel Livsey, Corwin Press Acquisitions Editor, for her editorial advice, support, and belief in me through this entire writing process. Her supportive, caring encouragement saw me through to the realization of this book.

I would also like to thank Editorial Assistant Phyllis Cappello, Production Editor Julia Parnell, and Copy Editor Diana Breti for all their help and encouragement.

Special acknowledgment is also due to Dr. Gay Fawcett, a colleague and dear friend, for originally empowering me to reach beyond my classroom walls.

The contributions of the following reviewers are gratefully acknowledged:

Marcella Emberger
Director
Maryland Assessment
    Consortium
Linthicum, MD

Lorraine M. Zinn
Senior Consultant
Lifelong Learning
    Options
Boulder, CO

Karen H. Peters
Senior Consultant
Kent State University
East Palestine, OH

Arthur L. Costa
Emeritus Professor of
    Education
California State
    University
Sacramento, CA

Michelle Collay
School Coach
Bay Area Coalition of
    Equitable Schools
Oakland, CA

Jennifer York-Barr
Associate Professor
University of Minnesota
Department of Educational
    Policy and Administration
Minneapolis, MN

Rosie O'Brien Vojtek
Principal
Ivy Drive Elementary School
Bristol, CT

Patricia B. Schwartz
Principal
Thomas Jefferson Middle School
Teaneck, NJ

Charles F. Adamchik, Jr.
Teacher/Educational
    Consultant
Blairsville High School and
    Learning Sciences
    International
Blairsville, PA

Dr. Germaine L. Taggart
Associate Professor
Fort Hays State University
Hays, KS

About the Author

 **Norene Bella** started her teaching career at Rootstown Elementary in Rootstown, Ohio, after graduating cum laude from Kent State University. She is currently a fourth-grade teacher in the Stow-Munroe Falls City School System in Stow, Ohio where she has also taught second and fifth grades. She is an innovative educator who, through a Martha Holden Jennings Foundation Grant, designed and implemented a unique technology classroom. Working with the local soil and water conservation department, she was instrumental in the development of an interactive learning habitat-nature realm at her school. Her students have benefited from many unique opportunities initiated by Miss Bella. She and her students have also been involved with the SBC Ameritech technology research classroom at Kent State University. She is a member of the National Education Association, Ohio Education Association, Kent State University Alumni Association, Kappa Delta Pi (International Honor Society in Education), Ohio's Coalition of National Board Certified Teachers, and Phi Delta Kappa (International Education Honorary Society). Attending the Milken Family Foundation's state of Ohio conferences has been an honor for Miss Bella. In 1997, Miss Bella was one of the first one hundred teachers in the state of Ohio to gain her National Board for Professional Teaching Standards certification. She has served as a National Board presenter and facilitator for Kent State University, Cleveland State University, Mount Union College, and Washington D.C. City Schools. She has presented at national education conferences on professional development and National Board certification. She is listed twice in *Who's Who Among America's Teachers.* In 1997, Miss Bella was honored with the State of Ohio Governor's Educational Leadership Award. She lives in Ohio with her family.

CORWIN
PRESS

The Corwin Press logo—a raven striding across an open book—represents the union of courage and learning. Corwin Press is committed to improving education for all learners by publishing books and other professional development resources for those serving the field of K–12 education. By providing practical, hands-on materials, Corwin Press continues to carry out the promise of its motto: "**Helping Educators Do Their Work Better**."

What Are the Benefits of Analyzing Student Work?

"**W**hat's in it for me?" That's the question many educators secretly ask themselves when they are presented with a new educational initiative, program, assessment tool, or resource material. Put in different words, they may ask, "How will this make me a better educator?" "Will this have an impact on my entire practice?" or, "How will this enhance my students' learning?" Yes, they might even ask, "How will this simplify my life?"

It is stating the obvious to say that educators are busy people. Within a normal week, when they are not with their students they may participate in at least one committee or staff meeting, make a dozen phone calls, spend an hour or two at the copy machine, gather resource materials, locate appropriate software or Internet sites to enhance their lessons, hold a parent conference, and participate in a staff development workshop. They might even find a few hours for their personal lives. It's no wonder they view any new initiative with a skeptical eye. How can they possibly find the time to try one more new approach when they are already caught up in the dailyness of teaching?

Teachers are responsible for the health and safety of their students, and increasingly, the teacher's role is being extended to include the social and emotional well-being of the students. Often teachers are so immersed in the immediacy of daily schedules, routines, and activities that it is easy for them to lose sight of their primary responsibility: to provide a safe, nurturing environment where students are engaged in relevant and memorable learning. However, committed educators must never lose sight of this primary responsibility; it is where educators need to focus their energy and commit their valuable time.

Additionally, teachers are all participants in some form of evaluation process. The process usually involves an external evaluator and classroom observation of a range of criteria, from the environment to the instructional strategies. While the intent of these evaluations is to improve and refine teacher practice, in fact they are primarily designed to comply with Board of Education policy. The evaluator usually focuses on teacher behavior rather than what the students are learning. At best, this type of evaluation affirms what teachers are doing well at that moment or offers constructive feedback for improvement. At worst, the evaluation is limited by the evaluator's knowledge of best practice. Evaluations are isolated in nature and focus primarily on teacher behavior within a limited time frame. Once the evaluation is completed, teachers rarely use the information gathered to plan for their individual growth or to improve student learning. While newer teachers may be observed annually, tenured teachers often teach several years without a formal classroom observation. With the development of teacher standards, cognitive coaching, peer review, and other such initiatives, the type of teacher evaluation described above is slowly vanishing, but unfortunately not quickly enough.

Regardless of the daily schedules, routines, activities, and the evaluation processes that consume so much time, educators need to focus their energy and commit their valuable time to their primary responsibility. Quality instruction cannot be left to chance after all the other responsibilities are attended to. The stakes are too high. Today's society demands that all students obtain the skills and attitudes necessary to be productive and contributing citizens. In order to be successful, students must have solid content knowledge. They must comprehend fundamental concepts and demonstrate their understanding in a variety of circumstances. Additionally, students must know how to begin and what processes to use when they are faced with new situations outside the classroom. This is the true purpose of learning. However, to successfully accomplish this, schools must be committed to helping educators shift the focus in all areas of their practices.

THE LEARNER-CENTERED CLASSROOM

Educators need to shift from teaching isolated content to promoting the development of essential thinking skills and processes that will equip their students to be lifelong learners. The Coalition of Essential Schools' (2002) first common principle for elementary and secondary schools defines it as "learning to use one's mind well." A shift from using textbooks as the primary source of content to emphasizing learning through real-life problem solving is needed. Students must be encouraged to constantly ask questions and seek answers, constructing and refining their knowledge base as they proceed. Experiences that enable students to self-assess, and to articulate their areas of strength and areas needing further attention, are vital to their academic growth. To support this type of process-oriented learning, teachers need to create classrooms in which interaction between students, and interaction between students and teacher, is valued—classrooms in which everyone works together and cooperative problem solving thrives. In this type of learner-centered classroom, the teacher shifts from being the leader on stage to being an expert, facilitator, and co-learner interacting and learning alongside the students. Educators need to focus their attention on these shifts in thinking in order to remain true to their primary commitment: to provide a safe, nurturing environment where their students are engaged in relevant and memorable learning that will continue throughout their lives. Teachers need to be thoughtful and deliberate when designing experiences for students. They need to carefully consider the content and process skills that are essential to their students' learning. Teachers need to provide experiences that are intellectually engaging and relevant to their students' lives. These experiences must be structured in a way that promotes self-directed learning.

At the same time, there is a need for an ongoing evaluation process to determine whether teachers are making these crucial shifts that are so vital to their students' futures. The evaluation process must reflect on student work to guide teachers' Professional Development Plans. Finally, due to the teachers' already overloaded agendas, the process must be easily incorporated into their daily practices. As Costa and Liebmann (1997c) state, "we are coming to understand that the act of teaching is a highly intellectual process involving continuous decision making—before, during, and after classroom instruction" (p. 37). They go on to state that these thought processes are influenced by deeply buried theories of learning, beliefs about education and student conduct, and teachers' cognitive styles.

THE COLLABORATIVE PROFESSIONAL DEVELOPMENT PROCESS

The Collaborative Professional Development Process is designed to take this highly complex and deeply buried thinking and raise it to a level of conscious decision making. It is a comprehensive approach to teaching that builds on understanding, designing, implementing, and examining student work. It focuses on the students for evidence of intellectual engagement. Educators using this process are able to design work that not only involves their students in activities but ensures that the activities are engaging their students' minds. Because of its reflective nature, the process allows educators not only to analyze the learning experiences they are designing for their students, but also to determine their effectiveness.

In discussions with teachers and administrators from seventeen school districts in Ohio, I found that truly committed professionals continually evaluate themselves. Highly successful educators discuss student progress with their colleagues and share ideas with each other. They believe that collegial discussions centered on teaching and learning have more impact on their practices than formal administrative observations. The administrators interviewed strongly agreed. Exemplary teachers believe in the power of collaboration so deeply that they will find the time for these dialogues. The challenge is to use this precious time in the most productive manner.

The Collaborative Professional Development Process was developed from discussions such as these, interviews with students and administrators, classroom observations, and traditional research. Five different sources of national standards of best professional practice were examined to design a Personal Teaching Inventory that encourages continual examination of a teacher's individual professional development. Costa and Liebmann's (1997a) research into indicators of intelligent behavior as well as Schlechty's (1997) research on effective Design Qualities of student work were studied. I conducted discussions with students of all ages to determine the conditions under which they believe they learn best. I also observed dozens of classrooms and discussed my observations with teachers and administrators. The findings were then synthesized into a powerful, reflective process that examines student work to inform teacher practice.

The Collaborative Professional Development Process is based on possibly the highest form of assessment—self-assessment—coupled with collegial support. The purpose throughout is to rethink, refine, and refocus teacher practices. The process is a cycle of self-assessment, collaborative analysis of student work, reflection, goal setting, and professional growth, as illustrated in Figure 1.1.

Although the process is self-evaluative, it recognizes the importance of collegial support. It is based on the belief that a teacher's colleagues can offer insights and alternative perspectives on student work, and consequently an essential component of the process is collaboration with one or more trusted colleagues. In Step 1, educators form collaborative learning teams. The teams initially meet to reach common understandings on crucial elements that will be used in the subsequent steps of the process. (For a description of the formation of collaborative learning teams, see Chapter 4.)

Step 2 is the completion of a Personal Teaching Inventory, to assess the degree to which the teacher has made the necessary shifts in lesson design, implementation strategies, analysis during instruction, and reflective practices to ensure process-oriented instruction. This inventory addresses a teacher's commitment to continued learning and growth, based on widely accepted standards of best practice: the Ohio Praxis Model (*Praxis III*, 1992), the *California Standards for the Teaching Profession* (1997), the National Board for Professional Teaching Standards (n.d.), and *Peer Assistance and Review* (2000). The inventory is a highly personal and confidential

Figure 1.1   Collaborative Professional Development Process

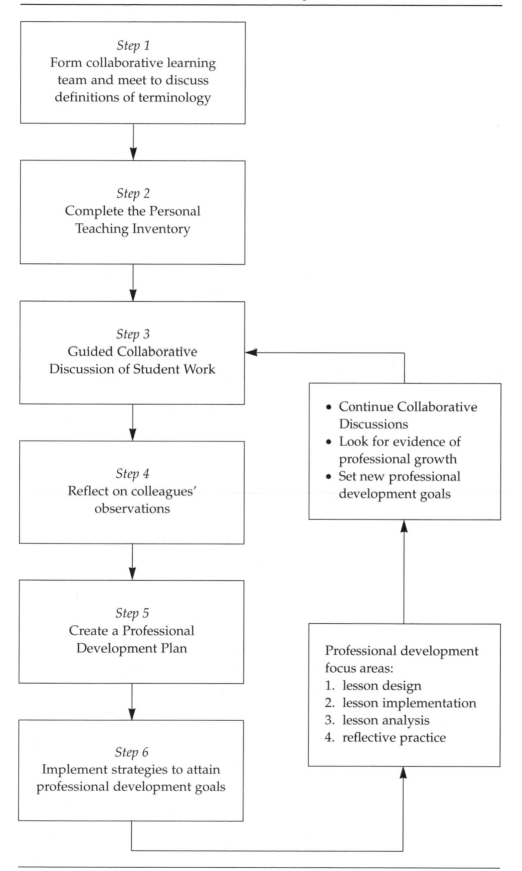

document. It calls for honesty and a willingness to critically examine oneself. Once the inventory is completed, educators become aware of the practice areas that need further attention. These areas will form the basis for their long-term Professional Development Plan. (For a detailed discussion of the Personal Teaching Inventory, see Chapter 4.)

Step 3 is the Guided Collaborative Discussion of Student Work, which is used to further define educators' areas of strength and the areas that need further attention in their practices. In fact, student work is at the very heart of the process. The structured discussion guides educators to look for evidence of Design Qualities and Intellectual Engagement Indicators in the work their students are producing. Like the *Looking at Student Work* (n.d.) initiative, an inquiry "stance" is very important at this point in the process. Educators are trying to learn from the student work, rather than trying to see what they think they already know. It elevates teachers' everyday discussions of classroom work to a level that will contribute to increased student learning and the teachers' personal and professional development. The Collaborative Professional Development Process zeroes in on the work designed by teachers and produced by their students as the true data to determine whether students are learning and the teachers' practices are effective. (A detailed description of the Guided Collaborative Discussion of Student Work is found in Chapter 5.) Teachers will also be pleased to know that these sessions can be accomplished in approximately thirty minutes; they can work in a trusting environment with their colleagues, within a timeframe of their own choosing. Moreover, they will have a sense of satisfaction as they watch their students accomplish their learning goals and become self-directed learners because of the shifts the teachers are making in their practices.

As the Collaborative Professional Development Process was developed, it became increasingly evident that self-assessment is extremely powerful when coupled with reflection. It is through reflection that educators adapt and expand their practices and pay special attention to their own professional development. As teachers expand their practices, they must also reflect on whether their students will be able to carry their learning into new situations when the teachers are no longer there to guide them. Teachers need to continually ask themselves whether their students have sufficient content and process skills to face new situations beyond the classroom walls. Step 4 emphasizes reflection. As part of the Guided Collaborative Discussion of Student Work, the teachers' trusted colleagues will offer their observations of the student work along with recommendations. Teachers may incorporate the recommendations into their practices if they so choose, but only after careful reflection on their appropriateness. Following these initial discussions, the teachers will complete Reflection Worksheets (see Chapter 5) and select samples of student work for their portfolios. On the Reflection Worksheet they will record any aspects of the discussions that are noteworthy. This is also the time for the teachers to reflect on the larger teaching purpose: will the work they are asking students to do enable them to apply what they've learned in situations outside the classroom walls?

During Step 5, teachers write a Professional Development Plan based on the Personal Teaching Inventory, the Collaborative Discussions of Student Work, and subsequent reflections. Teachers determine the practice area they would like to strengthen, and this becomes the focus of their Professional Development Plan. (Creating the Professional Development Plan is addressed in Chapter 6.)

In Step 6, educators work on their professional development goals. Educators will focus on one of four professional development areas: lesson design, lesson implementation, lesson analysis during instruction, or reflective practices. (The professional development focus areas are discussed in Chapters 7 through 9.) While working on their focus area, they continue to meet with their collaborative learning team to reflectively analyze student work samples. They look for evidence that their practices are being strengthened and that they are achieving their professional development goals. The evidence will be visible in their student work samples and will be recognized and commented on by their trusted colleagues during subsequent Collaborative Discussions of Student Work. The student work samples will be the benchmark of student and teacher growth.

After each subsequent Collaborative Discussion of Student Work, teachers will reflect on whether they have attained their professional development goals. As professional development goals are accomplished, other areas for improvement will be identified, and the teachers will revise their Professional Development Plans and set new professional development goals.

At this point the process becomes cyclic as teachers continue to set new goals; pursue professional development opportunities to study and strengthen the practice areas that need attention; look for evidence of growth by analyzing student work samples; and continue to reflect on, accomplish, and redefine goals to guide their professional development.

THE BENEFITS OF COLLABORATION

By using the Collaborative Professional Development Process, teachers will experience a depth of learning that can only occur in a truly collegial setting. They will have a running record of analysis, progress, changes, and thought patterns from which to build their practices. They will be using a formalized process that embodies the best practices of committed professionals, and that will guide them in planning for continual improvement. The process will enable them to equip their students for the "real" world and will achieve superior results for their students and for themselves as well.

Educators who use the Collaborative Professional Development Process have provided testimonials concerning its impact on their practices. They experience a newfound respect for each other as professionals. They realize that this process is not an add-on to their already busy professional lives, but is embedded in and enhances every aspect of their teaching. They see the value of a dynamic process that they will continue to use for the rest of their careers. One teacher said it succinctly: "The Collaborative Professional Development Process helps me plan for, not pray for, student success."

"What's in it for me?" teachers may still ask. Teachers, will it help your students take more responsibility for their own learning? Yes. Will it increase your effectiveness in the classroom? Yes. Will it promote your professional development? Yes. Will it simplify your lives? Yes. Well, at least it will allow you to use your valuable time in a more productive manner. Teaching and learning are complex processes and educators have limited time to analyze their practices. The Collaborative Professional Development Process is designed to be incorporated into the daily routines of all teachers. Teachers will find that it is an efficient method for analyzing and reflecting on student learning, and, as a result, their students will be more intellectually engaged in their work.

2

The Elements of Collaborative Analysis of Student Work

Teachers instinctively determine whether their daily instruction is successful or fails to meet the intended learning objectives. They may say to themselves, "Wow, that lesson really went well today," or "The students were really with me." Conversely, teachers may say, "What a disaster" or "I'll never do that again." As professionals, teachers are continually assessing the effectiveness of their instruction and the progress of their students. The question is: What standards are they using when they make their determination? Are they looking at standards-based criteria as they design their lessons? What are the standards for effective classroom instruction? How do teachers know that their students are truly intellectually engaged?

RECOGNIZED STANDARDS

Wong and Wong (1998) state that teachers are not in private practice. Each school district is owned by its local citizens. It has a set of policies and regulations that govern the behavior of all employees and students. The district's curriculum sets the goals for student learning. Teachers are accountable for the learning objectives that students must master at each grade level as they move toward successful completion of their K–12 experience. Wong

9

and Wong further state that teachers can no longer work in isolation, that they must have a common understanding of what students should know and how they should be able to demonstrate their concept mastery.

Long gone are the years when each teacher in isolation could determine the learning objectives. Education has moved from locally determined courses of study to statewide learning outcomes for all students. The federal government is even promoting a set of national standards, based on the premise that the expectations should be the same for all students no matter what state they happen to reside in. According to the Third International Mathematics and Science Study, "the current policy debates surrounding education encompass many issues, but debate at all levels (federal, state, and local) seems to place greatest emphasis on one area in particular: standards" (U.S. National Research Center, 1999). It is clear that teachers are being held more and more accountable to teach to local and state academic content standards and that their success as educators will be based on their students' success.

The Collaborative Professional Development Process is based upon recognized standards of best practice in education. The standards were synthesized and categorized according to appropriate teacher practice areas. They are based on an understanding of students' needs, interests, and abilities and take into account current research and practice. Pedagogical practice is evident throughout all the standards. The standards were organized according to the following five categories:

1. An Educator's Practice in the Presence of Students
   - Instruction is student focused
     - sets attainable, challenging standards
     - facilitates learning
     - challenges students to accept and share responsibility for their own learning
     - students use assessment criteria during the learning process
   - Contributes to building culture
     - clear and challenging expectations for learning and achievement
     - content is valued
     - pride in the work (students' and own)
   - Classroom community is student centered
     - encourages student inquiry, exploration, and questions
     - supports an atmosphere of cooperation and respect
     - knows students' names and interests
   - Student engagement is intellectual
   - Interaction is nurtured
     - student with student
     - student with teacher

2. An Educator's Practice in the Presence of Self (for benefit of students)
   - Is reflective
   - Critically examines practice and seeks opportunities for further study of subject matter and instructional strategies

- Adapts and expands practices to reflect new findings, ideas, and theories based upon experiences and research
- Contributes to the profession
- Embraces teaching with enthusiasm

3. An Educator's Practice in the Presence of Educational Colleagues
   - Student work is used as a basis for collaborative discussions about teaching and learning
   - Data is used to assess and improve student instruction
   - Colleagues collaboratively participate in structured reflection
   - Educators articulate and establish instructional goals and develop assessments that are congruent with building and grade level goals

4. An Educator's Practice in the Presence of Educational Structures
   - Plans and implements curriculum and instruction that follows district, state, and national models, employing current research and technology
   - Follows building procedures and routines that support student learning

5. An Educator's Practice in the Presence of Community
   - Upholds the standards of the teaching profession with community members, within and outside the school setting
   - Recognizes that community support validates quality student work

The Collaborative Professional Development Process concentrates on the development of the first three categories in an educator's practice. From these standards a Personal Teaching Inventory was created to determine a teacher's strengths and areas for growth (see Chapter 4). The process is based upon a collaborative, structured examination of student work. It is through this analysis that teachers can identify whether their students are moving toward concept mastery and what they can do to improve their students' chances of success.

As the Collaborative Professional Development Process was being developed, the revised staff development standards published by the National Staff Development Council were also closely examined. Their standard on collaboration states, "staff development that improves the learning of all students provides educators with the knowledge and skills to collaborate," and their standard on resources states, "staff development that improves the learning of all students requires resources to support adult learning and collaboration" (National Staff Development Council, 2001). This is the foundation that the Collaborative Professional Development Process rests on. It is based on a collaborative action research model and is embedded into the daily work of teachers. It organizes adults into learning communities. It uses student data to determine adult learning priorities, and it prepares educators to understand and appreciate all students.

If teachers are to hold students to higher standards and expectations, they must be willing to hold themselves to high standards and expectations. If teachers expect students to be more actively engaged in their learning, then teachers must be more actively engaged in their own learning. If teachers expect students to engage in relevant work, then teachers must engage in relevant work. If teachers believe in lifelong learning, then they must be living examples of that belief.

USING RESEARCH TO IMPROVE PRACTICE

During the development of the Collaborative Professional Development Process, I visited dozens of classrooms to look at the work students were doing. My goal was to identify the characteristics of quality assignments based on the level of intellectual engagement of the students. The premise was that, when students were truly engaged, it would be evident in their behavior and in the quality of work they produced. The types of work students were doing and the behavioral characteristics that indicated true interest and involvement in their assignments were charted. Discussions were held with highly regarded teachers about how they designed work for students and their observations of student engagement. Finally, students from kindergarten through high school were interviewed about the work they do and what excites them about learning. It didn't take long for patterns to emerge from these talks. Words like "purpose," "interesting," "relevant," and "chance to work with others" were repeated in all the student groups. Teachers spoke of students who were willing to work through assignments even when they were difficult. They spoke of students conferring with one another in order to compare findings. Teachers saw students refining and correcting in order to be more precise. They saw students asking relevant questions, asking "what if" questions, and thinking out loud at times. It became apparent that what the students and teachers were sharing was directly connected to the work of two important researchers: Dr. Arthur L. Costa and Dr. Phillip Schlechty.

"Regardless of the mode or style of learning, it is what students do and the meaning they give to what they do that determines what they learn" (Schlechty, 1997, p. 42). Much of Schlechty's research has focused on the work students do as a determining factor for successful schools. While the statement itself seems straightforward, it has far-reaching implications for the way schools are organized. Costa and Liebmann (1997a) state that "students entering the marketplace must come fully equipped with the skills that enable them to be lifelong learners. They must bring into the workplace their ability to think for themselves—to be self-initiating, self-modifying, and self-directing" (p. xiv). Costa and Liebmann have published a trilogy addressing the curriculum needs for the 21st century. The first book of the trilogy, *Envisioning Process as Content: Toward a Renaissance*

Curriculum, guided much of the thinking behind the Collaborative Professional Development Process.

The work of Costa, Liebmann, and Schlechty forms the basis for the Collaborative Professional Development Process. Their beliefs complement one another, and their research appears to be in alignment. These experts discuss the importance of designing work for students that will enable them to achieve the learning objectives as well as cope with confusing or ambiguous situations outside the classroom. Knowing how to behave when we don't know the answer is the true purpose of learning. Nothing is as important as engaging students in quality work that will teach them both content and process. This work must be so compelling that students will persist even when they find it difficult or demanding. The work must also produce a sense of satisfaction when it's completed—it must be rigorous and relevant. Costa, Liebmann, and Schlechty also analyze the processes by which knowledge is obtained and utilized, acknowledging that lesson design should focus on student performance rather than teacher performance. The Collaborative Professional Development Process centers on educator self-assessment that focuses on the work students do and the processes they develop. The work and the processes become the real measure of teacher success.

DESIGN QUALITIES

Schlechty (1997) has identified research-based criteria for designing quality work. He believes that, when student work is created using these criteria, the students will be more likely to engage the work, persevere, and find satisfaction in their schoolwork. Schlechty calls this set of criteria the Design Qualities:

- **Product Focus:** Work is clearly linked to some product. Students care about or see meaning in what they are asked to produce.
- **Clear and Compelling Product Standards:** Students are provided with clear criteria that they can use to assess their progress throughout the project.
- **Protection From Adverse Consequences:** Students are provided with feedback throughout the project, other than just at grade time. When a student fails to meet the standard, he or she is offered additional opportunities to complete the goal without the first effort affecting his or her grade.
- **Affirmation of Performance:** Products are made sufficiently public to others, rather than just the teacher.
- **Affiliation:** Tasks are designed in ways that encourage cooperative action among students and adults. The products are worthy of cooperative action to complete.
- **Novelty and Variety:** Products vary in kind, complexity, and length of time anticipated for completion. Tasks require students to use

new skills as well as new and different approaches, presentation styles, and modes of analysis.

- **Choice:** When choice in the product is limited, students are provided with a wide choice in the means of time, sequence, and order of steps. When the choice in time, sequence, and order is limited, students are provided with optimum choice in the products they will produce.
- **Authenticity:** Students believe that the quality of their product will have consequences for them. The product has significance and meaning to them. The conditions under which the work is done are similar to the "real" world.
- **Organization of Knowledge:** The knowledge that students are expected to master and use is organized in a way that is accessible and focused. Knowledge is presented in a way that allows students to see connections between disciplines. Students are provided with explicit instructions.
- **Content and Substance:** The content is culturally relevant. The work is aligned to the content that is required to be learned. The ideas, propositions, facts, and insights presented are consistent with those generally agreed upon by scholars in those disciplines. Content is appropriate to students' maturity level, experience, and background. It is presented in a way that is highly attractive to students.

These Design Qualities are based on the kind of work students indicated they are willing to do because it fundamentally motivates them. Schlechty (1997) further states that, if schools are not designing work that is engaging to students, then students will not learn what teachers, parents, and the community want them to learn. While he does not believe that students are teachers' products, he does believe that the work educators design for their students is. The students then become customers for this work, and it is often their choice as to how much effort they are willing to put into it. As teachers and their colleagues consider this list, it will be important to discuss the meaning of each Design Quality and to identify existing work that incorporates some of these qualities. It is important to note that these Design Qualities are intended to be a guide for lesson planning (see Chapter 7). As teachers determine what students should be able to do to demonstrate understanding, they should also determine which of the Design Qualities will increase the likelihood of engaging the students in the assignment. Schlechty would agree with those who say that sometimes the work we give students will be boring or routine, but he goes on to say that excitement and entertainment are not synonyms for a sense of accomplishment. Just as great performers are willing to experience the drudgery of daily practice in order to feel the sense of accomplishment when they perform publicly, so students will understand the necessity of routine work in order to feel a sense of satisfaction when using that work in a larger learning context.

INTELLECTUAL ENGAGEMENT INDICATORS

Costa and Liebmann (1997a) have researched the processes that are indicative of intelligent behavior and have identified three categories: skills, operations, and dispositions. Skills are discrete mental functions such as comparing and classifying or listening and asking questions. Operations are larger strategies performed over time; they are clusters of numerous skills. An example would be *communicating* as a compilation of both verbal and non-verbal skills such as attending, paraphrasing, and clarifying. Dispositions are habits of mind. Unlike skills, they are never fully mastered but are attitudes that seem to characterize the human will. Most importantly, Costa and Liebmann believe that dispositions can be taught and observed. They can be incorporated into the curriculum and encouraged and observed in the classroom. Dispositions are composed of thirteen attributes or character traits that teachers can teach to their students and observe in their classrooms when students are intellectually engaged:

• **Persistence:** Persevering when the solution to a problem is not readily apparent. Persistence means sticking to a task through to completion even though it may be difficult. It means having a systemic method for analyzing a problem.

• **Decreasing Impulsivity:** Thinking before taking action. Striving to clarify and understand directions or develop a strategy before tackling the problem. Effective people have a sense of deliberativeness.

• **Listening to Others With Understanding and Empathy:** The ability to listen to, empathize with, and understand someone else's point of view. Listening to others also involves being able to paraphrase another person's ideas and understanding others' feelings or emotional states.

• **Metacognition:** Awareness of our own thinking. Metacognition involves installing a plan of action before trying to solve a problem. It means consciously thinking about the plan while it's in progress in order to determine if it's working or it should be abandoned. It means to become increasingly aware of one's actions and their effects on others.

• **Striving for Accuracy and Precision:** Taking time to check over products, review the rules by which one is to abide, review the models and visions to follow, review criteria, and confirm that the finished product matches the criteria.

• **Questioning and Problem Posing:** Knowing how to ask questions to fill in the gaps between what one knows and what one doesn't know. It is the ability to find problems to solve. Effective questioners ask a range of questions. They recognize discrepancies and phenomena in their environment and search for their causes.

- **Drawing on Past Knowledge and Applying It to New Situations:** Being able to abstract meaning from one's experience, carry it forth, and apply it to new situations. Intelligent human beings learn from experience, calling on it to support, explain, or solve new challenges.

- **Displaying a Sense of Humor:** The ability to perceive situations from an original and interesting point of view. Humorous people thrive on finding incongruities and perceiving absurdities, ironies, and satire. It is being able to laugh at situations and themselves. Creative problem solvers have the ability to distinguish between situations of human frailty and fallibility where compassion is needed and situations that are truly funny.

- **Cooperative Thinking:** Knowing when it is important to spend time and energy on work that requires collective intelligence or physical ability. Working in groups requires the ability to justify ideas and to test the feasibility of solutions or strategies with one another. Working in cooperative groups requires the willingness to accept feedback from others.

- **Using All the Senses:** The ability to conceive and express many ways of solving problems by use of the senses: making observations, gathering data, experimenting, role playing, simulating, manipulating, visualizing, imitating, model building, and so on.

- **Ingenuity, Originality, Insight, Creativity:** The capacity to generate original, clever, and ingenious products, solutions, or techniques. Creative people are open to constructive criticism. They willingly hold up their products for others to judge and provide feedback so they can constantly refine their techniques.

- **Risk Taking:** Going beyond established limits. People who take risks place themselves in situations in which they do not know what the outcome will be. They can accept uncertainty, confusion, and a higher risk of failure as part of a normal process. They learn to view setbacks as interesting, challenging, and growth producing.

- **Wonderment, Inquisitiveness, Curiosity, and the Enjoyment of Problem Solving:** People who are filled with wonderment enjoy problem solving. They love making up problems to solve and request enigmas from others. They delight in figuring things out on their own and they continue to seek out situations to learn throughout their lifetimes.

Costa and Liebmann (1997a) state that this list is not meant to be complete and educators should constantly add to it based on their own observations of students. The Collaborative Professional Development Process relies heavily on reflection for both teachers and students, so a fourteenth attribute has been added:

- **Reflection:** Involves metacognition and encompasses the affective domain. It is the ability to identify feelings and emotions that accompany thinking. Reflection most often occurs at the completion of a task or activity; however, it is also useful at periodic points during the activity.

The Collaborative Professional Development Process was designed with the belief that with careful lesson design that incorporates the research of Schlechty, Costa, and Liebmann, students will be motivated to learn and develop the necessary dispositions that will take them into the 21st century as self-motivated and self-monitored adults. Costa and Liebmann's processes become the purpose of instruction and the subject of assessment. In the Collaborative Professional Development Process, these processes are referred to as the Intellectual Engagement Indicators. The Design Qualities become the criteria for the work educators design for students. The course content continues to be important in that students learn *from* the content not about it. The content is selected because of the important concepts it represents.

When educators incorporate Design Qualities and Intellectual Engagement Indicators into student work, thus increasing the quality of the work they design, they will increase the likelihood that students will be intellectually engaged and will produce high-quality work. The educators will be able to document the increase in quality through collaborative discussions (see Chapter 5). It will be evident not only in the work students produce but also in the behaviors they demonstrate as they work.

The research of Schlechty, Costa, and Liebmann and the standards described above are fundamental to the Collaborative Professional Development Process. Educators should make a commitment to learn more about the Design Qualities and the Intellectual Engagement Indicators and build this commitment into their Professional Development Plans. This can be done in a variety of ways: through study groups with colleagues, videotapes, and workshops or conferences based on the work of Schlechty and Costa. The bibliography contains many titles that educators will also find helpful.

3

Understanding Reflective Practice

This chapter concerns the power of reflection and its relationship to an educator's practice and the Collaborative Professional Development Process. Many people today realize the beneficial power of reflection in their personal and spiritual lives. Many books, magazine articles, and Internet sites can be found that explore the effect of reflection on the individual's personal and spiritual growth. The relationship between reflection and the educator's professional practice has also been studied, but it has not reached the popularity level of other areas of human development. As I have visited schools and observed numerous educators in action, I have come to realize that highly effective educators build some form of reflection into their daily practices. At the same time, from speaking with these educators I have come to realize that reflective practices also dominate their professional development endeavors. The Collaborative Professional Development Process has incorporated these two vital areas of reflection into the overall plan to strengthen teachers' practices. Chapter 6 discusses how reflection forms the basis of a teacher's Professional Development Plan. This chapter is devoted to reflection in general and explores how reflection is specifically related to a teacher's ability to evaluate the success of the lessons he or she has designed, implemented, and analyzed. The foundation of the Collaborative Professional Development Process is the ability of educators to be reflective in all aspects of their practices.

WHAT IS REFLECTIVE THINKING?

There are many definitions of reflective thinking. Most definitions include words such as inquiry, investigation, creativity, decision making, choices, and conclusions. Taggart and Wilson (1998) found these three commonalities to be present in most definitions: methodical process, inquiry orientation, and change or self-improvement as a goal (p. 17). Lasley (1992) states that reflection "refers to the capacity of a teacher to think creatively, imaginatively, and at times, self-critically about classroom practice" (p. 24). All teachers need to engage in this type of reflection daily to strengthen their practices. Reflection should be methodical, in that it should follow a pattern and become part of the teacher's daily routine. At the same time, reflection must be based on inquiry into the teacher's lesson designs, implementation strategies, and analytical skills. This type of reflection requires teachers to think imaginatively and creatively about every aspect of their practices. Finally, reflection must be carried out in a way that helps teachers realize that thinking critically about their practices does not diminish them as educators but elevates them to even greater heights when change or self-improvement is the goal.

MAKING TIME FOR DAILY REFLECTIVE PRACTICE

Talk in the teachers' lounge usually centers on sporting events, movies, and television programs everyone watched the night before. At the same time, when discussions happen to center on the educational endeavors of the teachers, often they are just as superficial. For many teachers, these short discussions are as far as they go in analyzing and reflecting on their daily practices. Unfortunately, this leads to very shallow teaching and very little development of the teachers' practices.

Chapter 9 addresses the importance of taking the time every day to analyze lessons. This analysis helps teachers to recognize the positive, productive parts of the lessons, and at the same time it illuminates the areas that need further attention. However, to stop there would result in little growth for the teachers or their students. After teachers have analyzed the lessons, reflection must take place. Daily reflection is something that many educators feel they have little or no time to indulge in. It is something that they only do in the dark of the night, as they lie awake in bed unable to sleep because of something that happened during their teaching that day. For others, reflective thoughts creep into their heads as they make the early morning commute to work, only to be interrupted by the blaring horn of the impatient driver next to them. Reflection is too important to be left to the stolen moments of the tired teacher's mind.

Teachers must schedule time every day to systematically reflect on the lessons they have taught that day. To do this for every lesson daily would be difficult, if not impossible, at first. In the beginning, teachers should choose a particular subject or class session to reflect on. As educators become more adept at reflective thinking, they will find that they can schedule more reflective thinking time into their daily practices and can reflect on more lessons during each session. Ultimately, the goal should be for teachers to reflect and adjust on the spot as they are teaching, not just when they set aside time for scheduled reflection. Ongoing and spontaneous reflection is what new teachers strive for and experienced teachers thrive on.

Some teachers find that keeping a reflective journal is helpful for developing their reflective skills and keeping track of areas for professional development. However, it is not essential for teachers to keep a daily reflective journal in order to use the Collaborative Professional Development Process. A reflective journal can be incorporated into teachers' practice when they feel ready to make the necessary time commitment. Figure 3.1 is a template for a journal page that can be placed in a reflective journal notebook. Educators will find this template especially helpful because it gives them a way to keep track of areas they may want to include in their Professional Development Plans.

THE REFLECTIVE THINKING CYCLE

There are many programs available that are designed to help teachers become more reflective. They lead the learner through the three modes of reflective thinking: technical, contextual, and dialectical. In-depth study of reflective thinking is not the purpose of this chapter. Instead, the purpose is to give teachers a starting point for reflective thinking, and by starting the practice of reflecting on their teaching, teachers can incorporate a structured study of reflection into their Professional Development Plans (see Chapter 6).

Dewey (1933), Eby and Kujawa (1994), Pugach and Johnson (1990), and Schon (1983) feel that the reflective thinking process follows a definite cycle. However, while they feel each cycle evolves from a problem, the Collaborative Professional Development Process is based on the premise that each cycle begins with either a problem or a high point. In the Collaborative Professional Development Process, the reflective thinking cycle begins with the **Focus Stage**. During this stage, teachers identify the problems that occurred during their teaching, as well as the high points— the parts of the lesson that went exceptionally well. The teachers record the problems and high points in their reflective journals (see Figure 3.1). Next, the teachers decide which problems or high points their reflective thinking will focus on. If the problem consumed the majority of the lesson time for the entire class or particular students, then that is what should be focused on. If overall the lesson went exceptionally well, or if particular students demonstrated exceptionally high levels of critical thinking skills, then that is where the immediate focus should be. This is not to contend that the

Figure 3.1   Reflective Journal Entry

Class: _____   **Date:** _____

Focus Stage: Problems and/or high points of the lesson.

_____

_____

Put an asterisk (*) next to the problem or high point that will be the focus of this reflective session.

Inquiry Stage: Begin with thought-provoking questions that help you clarify the problem or high point you have chosen to reflect on.

_____

_____

Referencing Stage: Search for similar problems and solutions or high points in past teaching experiences.

_____

_____

Strategy Stage: Document possible ways to solve the problem or duplicate the high point.

_____

_____

Implementation Stage: To be completed after implementing the above strategy. Document success or plans for future reflection and adjustments.

_____

_____

_____

items that are not chosen should just be forgotten. By recording them in their reflective journals, teachers can revisit them at a later time when their personal schedules permit. Once the focus point for the reflection has been identified, the reflective cycle advances to the **Inquiry Stage**.

The best way to begin the **Inquiry Stage** is with powerful and thought-provoking questions. The questions should be based on the initial analysis and the focus for reflection. These questions should be powerful enough to demand that teachers take the time to "step back" and examine their thinking.

- "How did my conscious modification during class help or hinder this student's learning?"
- "What personal biases or beliefs am I aware of when I call on more male than female students during science class?"
- "Why is writing a letter to the editor of the local newspaper an important skill for this child to learn?"
- "What other avenues might be more accessible for this student and accomplish the same result?"
- "Why is this relevant to this child's learning?"
- "How will this skill help the students today, tomorrow, next year, or in their adult lives?"
- "What made these few students advance to such a high level of critical thinking? Was it due to my presence in the room or was it self-motivated?"

Initial questions such as these help teachers clarify the problem or high point that they are focusing on. Next, the reflective teacher moves on to the **Referencing Stage**. It is at this point that teachers are compelled to go deeper and examine their own belief systems, value structures, and repertoires of past teaching experiences. At this stage, teachers try to make sense of the identified problems by searching for similar problems in their past teaching experiences. At the same time, they should also think about how solutions that worked in similar situations can be adapted to these new problems. Likewise, teachers will strive to reference the high point, if that is the focus of their reflections, to see whether the high point aligns with past experiences or is a unique experience that they want to reflect on further so it can become part of their teaching repertoires. If the problem the individual teacher has isolated parallels a past problematic situation, the teacher can choose to build on that experience and formulate possible solutions. If nothing in the teacher's past can serve as a reference, then he or she must be creative and imaginative and formulate new solutions. Similarly, if the high point that is being reflected on is a familiar one, then the teacher can duplicate it in future lessons. If it was a unique situation, the teacher must dissect it so the elements that created the powerful situation can be duplicated in the future, and it can ultimately become part of the teacher's repertoire.

The next step of the reflective thinking cycle involves developing a plan. This is the **Strategy Stage**. At this point the teacher develops

Figure 3.2   Reflective Thinking Cycle

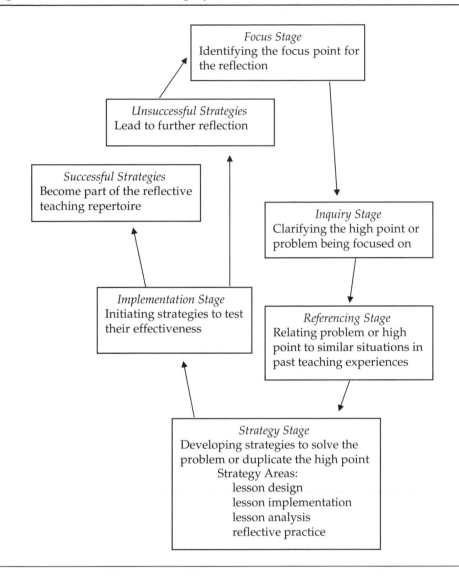

strategies to solve the problem or duplicate the high point. Teachers will find that these strategies involve modifying their lesson design, implementation strategies, or analysis. Next, the teacher initiates these strategies to test their effectiveness during the **Implementation Stage**. If the strategies are successful, they become part of the teacher's reflective teaching repertoire. If the strategies do not result in the intended outcome, the teacher must reflect on them further and begin the cycle all over again.

Over time, reflection helps teachers refine their philosophies and values about teaching and learning. It leads teachers to explore and refine their theoretical base and to align their practices with it daily. By using reflection to understand and adjust their practices, teachers build a base of reflective teaching strategies that supports their entire teaching practice. These reflective teaching strategies will permeate not only the teachers' practices but also those of other educators who come in contact with them.

Highly reflective teachers have much to share with those they mentor and teach with. They are influential because their expertise is grounded in thoughtful lesson design, implementation and analysis strategies, and reflection that compels them to constantly adjust and improve their practices.

In conclusion, teachers who think reflectively are highly successful educators in the classroom. They do not simply sigh with relief when things go well, and vow never to do something again when things do not go as planned in class. Instead, reflective teachers want to make sure they can duplicate the high points when there is a rich atmosphere in their classrooms and intellectual engagement is high. They also want to look closely at problems that impede the highest level of learning in their classrooms, so that the cause of the problem can be minimized in the future. Reflective teachers find the value in taking the time to reflect, focus, inquire, reference, and develop strategies to ensure that their own learning as educators never stops and their teaching only grows stronger.

4

Forming Collaborative Learning Teams

Educators engage in the Guided Collaborative Discussion of Student Work by forming collaborative learning teams. The teams can be teachers of the same grade level, teachers of the same content area, teachers and a principal, or simply a group of trusted colleagues with varied backgrounds who have a deep desire to work together professionally. No matter how the teams are configured, as long as the members are volunteers who have elected to work together to examine student work, the feedback will produce a discussion that will energize the participants unlike anything they have experienced before.

CHOOSING TEAM MEMBERS

It is essential to the Collaborative Professional Development Process that educators work with colleagues whom they respect and trust, in order to establish a safe environment in which to analyze and discuss student work. It is also essential that all the educators have the same commitment to the process. The process works best when three or four educators work together. This provides a variety of perspectives while still allowing for time management. Two colleagues can work together effectively; however, it limits the feedback. Just envision an entire staff becoming involved in the process. Imagine what a staff meeting could look like if the whole staff (divided into collaborative teams) met to discuss student work. Imagine the powerful level of intellectual engagement that would be present in the building.

As educators deliberate on how to form their collaborative learning teams, they should be aware that the team need not be limited to members of the same grade level or subject area. In fact, it can be very productive to vary the group's makeup. Some of the most powerful learning teams in Collaborative Professional Development workshops have been composed of educators in different grade levels and subject areas. The various group members bring new and unique perspectives to the discussions because of their different backgrounds.

Depending on the level of trust, newer educators and more experienced educators will benefit from working together. Experienced teachers can share insights based on their years of experience in the classroom, while beginning teachers can bring new perspectives and fresh ideas to the discussions. Mentor teachers and entry-level teachers may want to work together as part of their mentoring activities.

Educators who are considering National Board Certification will find that the Collaborative Professional Development Process will help to prepare them for both the portfolio and the assessment center portions of National Board Certification. As a National Board Certified teacher, I know how stimulating the certification process is. At the same time, many of the reflective processes I used to examine the work in my portfolio, and the resources I drew on when responding to the assessment center evaluation, have been incorporated into the Collaborative Professional Development Process. Educators who experience the Collaborative Professional Development Process will find they are well prepared for the demands of the National Board Certification endeavor.

In some cases, the Collaborative Professional Development Process will work well for cooperating teachers and their student teachers. Having worked with many student teachers over the years, I feel this process would add depth to discussions with student teachers about creating quality work for students. These discussions may lack the depth that more experienced teachers' discussions would have, but what a wonderful way to help new educators lay the foundations for their teaching practices. Right from their first days in the classroom, it would illustrate the power of lessons that are created around Schlechty's Design Qualities. At the same time, it would give the student teachers Intellectual Engagement Indicators to look for in their students, enabling them to recognize when intellectual engagement is thriving. Regardless of how educators structure their collaborative learning teams, the key is for them to work with people they trust and who are willing to look at student work with a critical friend's eye.

SETTING A SCHEDULE

Once educators have formed collaborative teams, they will need to select a regular time to meet. It is important to meet regularly and often so the sessions become embedded in daily practice. The Guided Collaborative Discussion of Student Work should be conducted at least once a month during the school year. Since the purpose is to inform the participating educators, the meetings should begin at a point in the school year when the routines of school are already established and findings may be successfully incorporated into future practice. If the sessions are attempted too early in the school year, they could produce anxiety on the part of the participating educators. If scheduled too late in the school year, the ability to bring about change could be reduced.

Certainly the more often these discussions are conducted, the more accepted, comfortable, and beneficial they will become for everyone involved. Frequent discussions will make people feel more familiar and will eventually result in a sense of professional teamwork. This will help to diminish teachers' feelings of vulnerability when their students' work is the source of the discussion. The more habitual the practice, the more advantageous it will be. Frequent discussions will result in a collegial group that has a heightened awareness of how an educator's plans translate into students' products—and in turn what that means to the educator's practice. Nothing can weaken a collegial group more than a member who is unwilling or unable to participate fully in the complete spectrum of the discussions. No matter what position a colleague holds in the building, no person should take a leadership role in which he or she leads the discussions yet never shares work. Trusted collegial groups of no more than four people should meet often enough that each educator is able to share his or her work at least four times during the year. It is advisable to have one guided discussion for each group member before featuring any teacher's work a second time. Depending on the time commitment of the team, several teachers' work may be featured at each session, making it possible for each teacher on the team to be featured numerous times throughout the year.

Due to the hectic schedules of most educators, the dialogue process was designed to take approximately one half hour. This allows for one person to present student work and receive feedback. The dialogue process does not have to add more work to the school day. For districts that hold staff meetings twice a month, a discussion of student work can be scheduled in place of one of the staff meetings. Alternatively, it can be held during regularly scheduled professional development days. For teachers who have team meeting periods, the discussion of student work could easily become a regular event. Inevitably, the discussions of student work will be the source of some truly elevated conversations about the work that is planned by the teachers on the team and produced by their students.

ESTABLISHING COMMON DEFINITIONS

Before the members of the team begin the Guided Collaborative Discussion of Student Work, they must agree on definitions of terminology. Often people think they have the same understanding of terminology, but when they begin to explore meaning they find that definitions can be very different. The collaborative learning team must agree on the meaning of terms before they can effectively discuss student work. The first few meetings of a collaborative learning team are devoted to establishing these common understandings. The three areas that require agreement on definitions of terminology are the lesson Design Qualities, Intellectual Engagement Indicators, and the standards that the Collaborative Professional Development Process is built on. Figure 4.1 is a worksheet that team members can use to start their discussion of the definitions of Intellectual Engagement Indicators and Design Qualities. Figures 4.2 through 4.5 are examples of worksheets completed by teachers using the Collaborative Professional Development Process. After completing the worksheets, the team members should discuss their understanding of the terms so that group definitions start to emerge. Team members may find this difficult at first, but it will become easier as they grow to understand and use the Design Qualities and Intellectual Engagement Indicators in their own teaching and discuss them in their collaborative learning teams. This is only a starting point, and further study can be incorporated into individual teachers' Professional Development Plans as well.

To function productively, the collaborative learning team also needs to establish a common understanding of the standards that the Collaborative Professional Development Process is based on. These standards were introduced in Chapter 2, but appear here in a concise document with the Collaborative Professional Development Process components included. Figure 4.6 begins with a statement of personal commitment to professional practice and includes the complete list of standards. Figures 4.7 through 4.9 are worksheets that will help collaborative learning teams begin their discussion and understanding of the first three standards. Each member of the collaborative team should fill out a worksheet documenting the team's definitions of terminology and questions. The worksheets can then be referred to in future team meetings and can be used when the team members are working through their individual inventories on their own. Figures 4.10 through 4.12 are examples of worksheets that were completed by Collaborative Professional Development team members.

(Text continues on page 42)

Figure 4.1   Intellectual Engagement Indicator Worksheet

1. Indicator of Intellectual Engagement to be discussed:

_____

_____

_____

2. What does this Intellectual Engagement Indicator mean?

_____

_____

_____

3. What would this indicator look like in the classroom?

_____

_____

_____

4. Which Design Qualities embedded in the lesson/unit design would result in students being intellectually engaged, as evidenced by the Intellectual Engagement Indicator discussed above?

_____

_____

_____

_____

Figure 4.2 Sample Intellectual Engagement Indicator Worksheet

1. Indicator of Intellectual Engagement to be discussed:

   Persistence

2. What does this Intellectual Engagement Indicator mean?

   When students stick with an assignment even when problems arise and it becomes difficult. Students trying different strategies to solve a problem situation before they ask for help from teachers or peers. Students following through with work and trying hard to produce quality work.

3. What would this indicator look like in the classroom?

   There would be sufficient materials and time available to the students to try alternative strategies to solve problems. Students would be given some choices in the assignments they are given. Students would be working interdependently. Initial failures would not count against a student's grade.

4. Which Design Qualities embedded in the lesson/unit design would result in students being intellectually engaged, as evidenced by the Intellectual Engagement Indicator discussed above?

   1. Organization of Knowledge

   2. Choice

   3. Affiliation

   4. Protection From Adverse Consequences

Figure 4.3   Sample Intellectual Engagement Indicator Worksheet

1. Indicator of Intellectual Engagement to be discussed:

   Decreasing Impulsivity

2. What does this Intellectual Engagement Indicator mean?

   The ability to think things through before taking action. Students who take
   the time to carefully consider assignments and think about how they are
   going to accomplish them before they begin to work. Students do not act in
   haste.

3. What would this indicator look like in the classroom?

   Time would be allotted for students to question and clarify the directions and
   meaning of the assignment before they begin. Students would be planning
   and reflecting before beginning long-term projects. Assessment rubrics would
   be shared with or created by students. The classroom would resemble "real
   life" conditions so students could make the connection between the work and
   the "real world."

4. Which Design Qualities embedded in the lesson/unit design would result in
   students being intellectually engaged, as evidenced by the Intellectual
   Engagement Indicator discussed above?

   1. Product Focus

   2. Authenticity

   3. Clear and Compelling Product Standards

Figure 4.4 Sample Intellectual Engagement Indicator Worksheet

1. Indicator of Intellectual Engagement to be discussed:

   Listening to Others with Understanding and Empathy

2. What does this Intellectual Engagement Indicator mean?

   Students would know how to listen to others. They would be able to pick up on the other person's ideas, feelings, attitudes, and emotions. They would be able to understand another person's opinions and they would be able to empathize with them.

3. What would this indicator look like in the classroom?

   Students would be working interdependently. Students would be encouraged to be aware of the feelings and emotional states of others through their verbal cues and body language. Good listening skills would be modeled and praised. Students would be paraphrasing, building on the ideas and feelings, clarifying and giving examples after listening to the ideas of others.

4. Which Design Qualities embedded in the lesson/unit design would result in students being intellectually engaged, as evidenced by the Intellectual Engagement Indicator discussed above?

   1. Affiliation

   2. Protection From Adverse Consequences

   3. Clear and Compelling Product Standards

Figure 4.5   Sample Intellectual Engagement Indicator Worksheet

1. Indicator of Intellectual Engagement to be discussed:

   Striving for Accuracy and Precision

2. What does this Intellectual Engagement Indicator mean?

   Students who check over their work to make sure they have followed the rules and criteria. They can defend their work and explain why they completed the work in the way that they did.

3. What would this indicator look like in the classroom?

   Students would be checking over the rules, procedures, criteria, and models throughout to make sure their work was accurate. They would be given time to make adjustments if necessary. They would be explaining their rationale and judgments in both oral and written forms.

4. Which Design Qualities embedded in the lesson/unit design would result in students being intellectually engaged, as evidenced by the Intellectual Engagement Indicator discussed above?

   1. Content and Substance

   2. Novelty and Variety

   3. Affirmation of Performance

Figure 4.6   Standards of the Collaborative Professional Development Process

A Personal Commitment to Professional Practice

Educators must affirm that standards are required by their profession. This commitment demands that standards be practiced rather than just acknowledged.

Standards

1. An Educator's Practice in the Presence of Students

   Collaborative Professional Development Process components: Lesson Design/Embedding the Design Qualities, Implementation, and Analysis

   - Instruction is student focused

     – sets attainable, challenging standards

     – facilitates learning

     – challenges students to accept and share responsibility for their own learning

     – students are aware of and create criteria by which their work will be assessed

   - Contributes to building culture

     – clear and challenging expectations for learning and achievement

     – content is valued

     – pride in the work (students' and own)

   - Classroom community is student centered

     – student inquiry, exploration, and questions are encouraged

     – supports an atmosphere of cooperation and respect

     – knows students' names and interests

   - Student engagement is intellectual (as evidenced by the presence of Intellectual Engagement Indicators)

   - Interaction is nurtured

     – student with student

     – student with teacher

2. An Educator's Practice in the Presence of Self (for the benefit of students)

   Collaborative Professional Development Process components: Reflective Practices, Implementation, and Analysis

   - Is reflective

   - Critically examines practices and seeks opportunities for further study of subject matter and instructional strategies

   - Adapts and expands practices to reflect new findings, ideas, and theories based upon experiences and research

   - Contributes to the profession

   - Embraces teaching with enthusiasm

3. An Educator's Practice in the Presence of Educational Colleagues

   Collaborative Professional Development Process components: Reflective Practices, Guided Collaborative Discussions of Student Work

   - Student work is used as a basis for collaborative discussions about teaching and learning

   - Data is used to assess and improve student instruction

   - Colleagues collaboratively participate in structured reflection

   - Educators articulate and establish instructional goals and develop assessments that are congruent with building and grade-level goals

4. An Educator's Practice in the Presence of Educational Structures

   - Plans and implements curriculum and instruction that follow district, state, and national models employing current research and technology

   - Follows building procedures and routines that support student learning

5. An Educator's Practice in the Presence of Community

   - Upholds the standards of the teaching profession with community members, within and outside the school setting

   - Recognizes that community support validates quality student work

Figure 4.7   Collaborative Learning Team Standards Worksheet 1

1. An Educator's Practice in the Presence of Students

(Lesson Design/Embedding the Design Qualities, Implementation, and Analysis)

❖ Instruction is student focused
 	
    • sets attainable, challenging standards
 	
    • facilitates learning
 	
    • challenges students to accept and share responsibility for their own learning
 	
    • students are aware of and/or create criteria by which their work will be assessed	

❖ Contributes to building culture
 	
    • clear and challenging expectations for learning and achievement
 	
    • content is valued
 	
    • pride in the work (students' and own)	

❖ Classroom climate/community is student centered
 	
    • student inquiry, exploration, and questions are encouraged
 	
    • supports an atmosphere of cooperation and respect
 	
    • knows students' names and interests	

❖ Student engagement is intellectual *(as evidenced by the presence of Intellectual Engagement Indicators)*	

❖ Interaction is nurtured
 	
    • student with student
 	
    • student with teacher	

Figure 4.8 Collaborative Learning Team Standards Worksheet 2

2. An Educator's Practice in the Presence of Self (for the benefit of students)

(Reflective Practices, Implementation, and Analysis)

❖ Educators are reflective	
❖ Educators critically examine their practice and seek opportunities for further study of subject matter and instructional strategies	
❖ Educators adapt and expand practices to reflect new findings, ideas, and theories based upon experiences and research	
❖ Educators contribute to the profession	
❖ Educators embrace teaching with enthusiasm	

Figure 4.9   Collaborative Learning Team Standards Worksheet 3

3. An Educator's Practice in the Presence of Educational Colleagues

(Reflective Practices, Guided Collaborative Discussions of Student Work)

❖ Student work is used as a basis for collaborative discussions about teaching and learning	
❖ Data is used to assess and improve student instruction	
❖ Colleagues collaboratively participate in structured reflection	
❖ Educators articulate and establish instructional goals and develop assessments that are congruent with building and grade-level goals	

Figure 4.10 Sample Collaborative Learning Team Standards Worksheet 1

1. An Educator's Practice in the Presence of Students

(Lesson Design/Embedding the Design Qualities, Implementation, and Analysis)

❖ Instruction is student focused • sets attainable, challenging standards • facilitates learning • challenges students to accept and share responsibility for their own learning • students are aware of and/or create criteria by which their work will be assessed	• Set the standards so students are challenged. Make the standards clear to all students. Let students know you feel they are capable of achieving at a high level of intellectual engagement. • Rotate teacher roles: facilitator, expert, co-learner. • Allow students to help create rubrics and other assessments.
❖ Contribute to building culture • clear and challenging expectations for learning and achievement • content is valued • pride in the work (students' and own)	• All content is valued. Praise the work of all students even other grade levels.
❖ Classroom climate/community is student centered • student inquiry, exploration, and questions are encouraged • supports an atmosphere of cooperation and respect • knows students' names and interests	• Encourage open participation and questioning. Praise students' efforts. • Let students know you are personally interested in them.
❖ Student engagement is intellectual *(as evidenced by the presence of Intellectual Engagement Indicators)*	• Teachers should have a list of Intellectual Engagement Indicators with them when teaching so they can look for those they embedded in their lesson designs.
❖ Interaction is nurtured • student with student • student with teacher	• Encourage and give students time to interact with peers and teachers.

Figure 4.11 Sample Collaborative Learning Team Worksheet 2

2. An Educator's Practice in the Presence of Self (for the benefit of students)

(Reflective Practices, Implementation, and Analysis)

❖ Educators are reflective	• Educators should take the time to reflect daily—both structured and unstructured reflection.
❖ Educators critically examine their practice, and seek opportunities for further study of subject matter and instructional strategies	• Educators should see the value in reflecting on the areas that they need to strengthen as well as those that are very strong. They should seek out opportunities and attend workshops, classes, and seminars to strengthen weak areas or areas that they would like to explore.
❖ Educators adapt and expand practices to reflect new findings, ideas, and theories based upon experiences and research	• Educators should constantly refine their practices as they gain experience. Educators should be aware of current research.
❖ Educators contribute to the profession	• Educators should find their areas of expertise and find ways they can contribute to the teaching profession, for example, writing journal articles, mentoring, acting as grade-level chairpersons, etc.
❖ Educators embrace teaching with enthusiasm	• Educators should show the enthusiasm of lifelong learners, constantly modeling for their students.

Figure 4.12   Sample Collaborative Learning Team Standards Worksheet 3

3. An Educator's Practice in the Presence of Educational Colleagues

(Reflective Practices, Guided Collaborative Discussions of Student Work)

❖ Student work is used as a basis for collaborative discussions about teaching and learning	• Educators should not teach in isolation. They should seek out opportunities to talk with other educators about teaching and learning. • Student work samples should be used as the basis of these talks.
❖ Data is used to assess and improve student instruction	• The student work should be assessed using the Design Qualities and Intellectual Engagement Indicators. • The data from these assessments should be used to improve the teachers' practices, thus improving student instruction.
❖ Colleagues collaboratively participate in structured reflection	• Educators should incorporate time to reflect with their colleagues.
❖ Educators articulate and establish instructional goals and develop assessments that are congruent with building and grade level goals	• Instructional goals should be established based on the Intellectual Engagement Indicators and Design Qualities. Educators should be able to articulate these goals and develop assessments that align with them and with building/grade-level goals.

COMPLETING THE PERSONAL TEACHING INVENTORY

Step 2 of the Collaborative Professional Development Process is completion of the Personal Teaching Inventory (Figures 4.13 through 4.15). Educators must remember that this is a personal inventory, even though they have already discussed the three standards with their collaborative learning teams. All educators must determine whether or not they meet each standard at this point in their professional journeys. It is important for them to be honest with themselves and document how they meet each standard. There is also space for educators to record any questions that arise as they examine the standards, for example, questions concerning their understanding of the standard or the evidence needed for documentation. The real purpose of this inventory is to begin a reflective inner dialogue and record their thoughts for the future. The goal for educators is to identify areas in which they want to grow and improve their understanding. The measure of whether they are meeting the goals will be the work their students produce. Figures 4.16 through 4.18 show how one teacher completed this inventory when she started the Collaborative Professional Development Process.

SELECTING STUDENT WORK

When people redecorate a room, they begin by taking inventory. They look over the items they have and decide what they will need to transform the look and feel of the room. Rarely do they eliminate all the furniture, but instead they decide which pieces of furniture will be kept and incorporated into their new design. These pieces become the foundation, and new furnishings are added to complete the new look. The Personal Teaching Inventory is similar to redecorating a room. As educators complete the inventory, they undoubtedly will find evidence of many impressive standard practices, and at the same time they will see areas that could use some "fixing up." Just as a room can display an individual's decorating expertise, student work can provide evidence of a person's practice as an educator. Looking for evidence in the great variety of student work is a worthwhile venture that can lead to powerful insights into the depths of an educator's practice.

Student work appears in many forms and serves many purposes: children share their work with their parents as proof of their hard work; teachers use students' work as a basis for parent/teacher discussions and to document grades; student work samples are evaluated for many state-mandated assessments. Student work is collected in portfolios to document their growth over a period of time and is displayed at various functions for the rest of the school to appreciate and enjoy. Newsletters feature the most recent classroom endeavors, articles are published in hometown newspapers, videotapes of classroom activities are played at an

(Text continues on page 49)

Figure 4.13   Personal Teaching Inventory – Standard 1

Taking a Personal Inventory: Where Am I?

1. An Educator's Practice in the Presence of Students

    (Lesson Design/Embedding the Design Qualities, Implementation, and Analysis)

	Evidence of:	Questions I have:
❖ Instruction is student focused • sets attainable, challenging standards • facilitates learning • challenges students to accept and share responsibility for their own learning • students are aware of and/or create criteria by which their work will be assessed		
❖ Contributes to building culture • clear and challenging expectations for learning and achievement • content is valued • pride in the work (students' and own)		
❖ Classroom climate/community is student centered • student inquiry, exploration, and questions are encouraged • supports an atmosphere of cooperation and respect • knows students' names and interests		
❖ Student engagement is intellectual *(as evidenced by the presence of Intellectual Engagement Indicators)*		
❖ Interaction is nurtured • student with student • student with teacher		

Figure 4.14 Personal Teaching Inventory – Standard 2

Taking a Personal Inventory: Where Am I?

2. An Educator's Practice in the Presence of Self (for the benefit of students)

(Reflective Practices, Implementation, and Analysis)

	Evidence of:	**Questions I have:**
❖ Educators are reflective		
❖ Educators critically examine their practice and seek opportunities for further study of subject matter and instructional strategies		
❖ Educators adapt and expand practices to reflect new findings, ideas, and theories based upon experiences and research		
❖ Educators contribute to the profession		
❖ Educators embrace teaching with enthusiasm		

Figure 4.15   Personal Teaching Inventory – Standard 3

Taking a Personal Inventory: Where Am I?

3. An Educator's Practice in the Presence of Educational Colleagues

(Reflective Practices, Guided Collaborative Discussions of Student Work)

	Evidence of:	Questions I have:
❖ Student work is used as a basis for collaborative discussions about teaching and learning		
❖ Data is used to assess and improve student instruction		
❖ Colleagues collaboratively participate in structured reflection		
❖ Educators articulate and establish instructional goals and develop assessments that are congruent with building and grade level goals		

Figure 4.16   Sample Personal Inventory – Standard 1

Taking a Personal Inventory: Where Am I?

1. An Educator's Practice in the Presence of Students

(Lesson Design/Embedding the Design Qualities, Implementation, and Analysis)

	Evidence of:	Questions I have:
❖ Instruction is student focused • sets attainable, challenging standards • facilitates learning • challenges students to accept and share responsibility for their own learning • students are aware of and/or create criteria by which their work will be assessed.	• National Math Council Standards • COS Standards • I ask leading questions • Students have choice in most assignments. • Students are aware of grading rubrics.	• Am I the leader too often? • How can I give students more choice? • Should students create rubrics?
❖ Contributes to building culture • clear and challenging expectations for learning and achievement • content is valued • pride in the work (students' and own)	• Multi-leveled instruction to challenge all students. • Connect content to real world.	• Is process viewed as valued content?
❖ Classroom climate/ community is student centered • student inquiry, exploration, and questions are encouraged • supports an atmosphere of cooperation and respect • knows students' names and interests	• Most lessons are inquiry based. • Encourage cooperation with team point system. • Participation rubrics. • Lunch Bunch – sharing	
❖ Student engagement is intellectual *(as evidenced by the presence of Intellectual Engagement Indicators)*	• Students exhibit higher-level thinking skills.	• How can I be sure all students are thinking at a high level?
❖ Interaction is nurtured • student with student • student with teacher	• Encourage both interdependent and individual work. • Try to be very available to students.	• Could I be more of a co-learner?

Figure 4.17 Sample Personal Inventory – Standard 2

Taking a Personal Inventory: Where Am I?

2. An Educator's Practice in the Presence of Self (for the benefit of students)

(Reflective Practices, Implementation, and Analysis)

	Evidence of:	Questions I have:
❖ Educators are reflective	• At the end of the day I try to evaluate the good and the bad parts of my day. • I try to incorporate the things that make some of my lessons very successful.	• Should I be doing more? Reflective journaling perhaps?
❖ Educators critically examine their practice and seek opportunities for further study of subject matter and instructional strategies	• I attend workshops and classes to strengthen the areas I think are weak.	• Do I tend to attend only in the areas that interest me?
❖ Educators adapt and expand practices to reflect new findings, ideas, and theories based upon experiences and research	• I have incorporated a lot more technology in my lessons over the past few years.	• Have I made adjustments in all areas?
❖ Educators contribute to the profession	• I serve as a mentor teacher. • I serve on textbook review committees. • I worked on the technology course of study.	
❖ Educators embrace teaching with enthusiasm	• I try to be a positive role model for my students and try to share a love of learning with them.	• What are some new things I could do to convey this?

Figure 4.18 Sample Personal Inventory – Standard 3

Taking a Personal Inventory: Where Am I?

3. **An Educator's Practice in the Presence of Educational Colleagues**

(Reflective Practices, Guided Collaborative Discussions of Student Work)

	Evidence of:	**Questions I have:**
❖ Student work is used as a basis for collaborative discussions about teaching and learning	• Student work is reviewed when I recommend students for testing when they are having problems.	• Why doesn't our team review student work for reasons other than testing?
❖ Data is used to assess and improve student instruction	• Very little. Only quick comments made in the hall between classes.	
❖ Colleagues collaboratively participate in structured reflection	• I don't feel I have ever done collaborative structured reflection.	• How would we even start?
❖ Educators articulate and establish instructional goals and develop assessments that are congruent with building and grade-level goals	• Articulate goals, etc. more with parents than I do with colleagues.	• How could we incorporate time for collaborative discussions?

Open House, and Web site postings expose student work to an even broader community. But the work can serve one more important purpose: student work can tell *all* educators about the inner workings of *their own* individual practices.

Imagine the student work standing alone. What does it say without explanation or discussion? Other than providing evidence of the content, class, and student, what does it say about the educator who designed it? How can it inform the educators about their practices? In fact, having the work stand on its own, without explanation, is the beginning of a specially structured discussion of student work. That is the shift in focus that is the heart of the Collaborative Professional Development Process. It uses the work that was designed by educators and produced by their students as the focus for professional discussions and professional development. It is the collaborative examination of the work that will inform educators about their practices and lead them to strengthen and build on their foundations.

During each collaborative learning team meeting, at least one educator's work samples are the focus of the discussion. It is recommended that the teacher select the work of four students representing a range of ability. Two students should be of similar ability. Using these same four students' work samples during subsequent sessions will ensure two things: it will provide the presenting teacher with insight into the impact the Collaborative Professional Development Process has on individual students, and it will demonstrate to the other team members how this process affects students of all levels of ability.

Student names should be removed from the work samples and the samples should be labeled numerically for identification purposes. If the work sample includes pictures or a video of students, student and parental consent must be obtained prior to sharing it with other staff members.

At first thought, teachers might be tempted to bring the most flawless samples of their most tried and true assignments for the session. There might be some hesitation about bringing less-than-successful work samples to be shared with colleagues, but it is important to remember why this discussion is being held. It is not intended to be a display of only the best work produced by the most talented students. It is an attempt to examine typical student work samples for evidence of the Design Qualities and Intellectual Engagement Indicators. Additionally, work samples do not have to be culminating projects of major units. Work samples that represent typical daily assignments are excellent artifacts to use as a basis for discussion. Certainly the majority of the work students are asked to complete is of this category.

In fact, the work brought for examination does not have to be tangible at all. Videotapes of student discussions or group work are wonderful examples of student work in action—imagine watching a student defending the strategies he or she used to solve a mathematical problem, or consider the impact of viewing a group of students participating in a social studies simulation. All educators can learn from the practices of performing and visual arts teachers. The work of their students is always a source of discussion due to its public nature; as the work is produced it is displayed and discussed for the benefit of all involved. What are some other examples of students displaying observable intellectual engagement? What does it look like?

- Imagine a classroom discussion in which students are able to actively listen to each other. They are able to summarize the speaker's words. Through active listening they are able to reach a consensus as a group.
- Picture students working on a new computer program. They realize they are limited in their ability to proceed smoothly and accept setbacks as a normal part of learning. Their display of insight into the situation is an example of intellectual engagement.
- Students whose approach to a new task is to take their time in the planning stage to thoroughly think through the various steps they intend to undertake are demonstrating a high degree of metacognition. They realize they need to think before taking action.
- When students are faced with logic puzzles or deductive reasoning scenarios, the answer is rarely obvious. When one attempt to solve the puzzle is not successful, an alternative strategy is tried. This is a display of persistence, an indicator of intellectual engagement.
- When conducting experiments in science, students pose solutions to problems in order to see if their hypothesis is realistic. If the results are not as expected, students probe the causes of the problem and investigate new ideas as a way of being engaged intellectually.
- Students who can cite examples from their own experiences that connect to characters in a story are involved intellectually. They understand the relevance of the reading to their lives.
- When students are able to understand the subtleties of irony, they have acquired the intellectual trait of scholarly humor.

Many of these examples are displayed daily in classrooms everywhere. But how can educators make these situations more predictable? Teachers need to share their work with other professionals to learn from one another and to identify and reinforce these situations. Participating in Guided Collaborative Discussion of Student Work can accomplish this.

5

Guiding Collaborative Discussion of Student Work

Once the collaborative learning team has prepared for the Guided Collaborative Discussion of Student Work (as described in Chapter 4) and is ready to proceed, the following step-by-step guide will help even the very first discussion to be successful and productive. There are six steps in the Collaborative Discussion of Student Work, and they should be followed as closely as possible (see Figure 5.1).

STEP 1: PRESENTATION OF STUDENT WORK

Probably the most difficult step to address is Step 1. Without making comment, the presenting teacher shares samples of selected student work. It only seems natural to explain the details of an assignment, but if an explanation of the assignment precedes the observation of the work, colleagues will have a preconceived notion of what they are expected to see. It will actually restrict their unbiased observation of the work. Because they are trusted colleagues, it is likely that they will find evidence of the original intent of the lesson. They might even see evidence of Design Qualities or

Intellectual Engagement Indicators that the presenting teacher did not consciously plan for when designing the work. As the trusted colleagues use the Observation Worksheet (Figure 5.2) to guide their observations, they will be reminded to look for evidence of Design Qualities and Intellectual Engagement Indicators. But if an explanation is given beforehand by the presenting teacher, it will color the viewing of the work samples. Once again, the work must stand alone. This method allows the areas of strength to shine through. If the work does not display what the presenting educator intended, that too is important. In fact, it is during this process of examining work designed for students that educators will be able to assess the areas needing additional professional development. Over time, the students' work will build a body of evidence of areas of strength and areas needing further development in the presenting educator's practice.

STEP 2: COLLEAGUES' OBSERVATIONS OF STUDENT WORK

In Step 2, the colleagues observe and describe the student work. Just as the presenting teacher has to refrain from explaining the work that is being presented, the trusted colleagues need to resist the urge to praise or ask questions about what they are observing. It is a task that sounds simple but actually is challenging. If everyone remembers that this experience has an objective and a recommended time limit, it will help the pace of the session. Observations should be made in descriptive, non-evaluative terms. Nothing should be inferred. If the work is a videotape of a literature circle involving four students, that is what should be stated. If it is a research paper written by one individual, that is how it should be described.

Evidence of Design Qualities should be noted. For example, if colleagues are observing samples of the research paper mentioned above, they might note that the teacher had "Clear and Compelling Product Standards" as a Design Quality, evidenced by the specific details that were contained in all the samples. Evidence of Intellectual Engagement Indicators should also be identified. For example, while viewing a videotape of the literature circle mentioned above, a colleague could note that students were able to paraphrase another student's comments. This is an example of the Intellectual Engagement Indicator "Listening to Others with Understanding and Empathy." Once again, if the colleagues write their comments on the Observation Worksheet (Figure 5.2), it should help focus their efforts and guide their verbal comments and observations. Figure 5.3 is a quick reference chart of the Design Qualities and Intellectual Engagement Indicators that may be helpful during this step of the process. This step should take approximately one third of the session time.

STEP 3: PRESENTING TEACHER'S RESPONSE

In Step 3, the presenting teacher has an opportunity to talk for the first time. There are five statements that he or she completes as an explanation of the work that was brought to the session:

1. The purpose of this assignment was . . .

2. This assignment connects to the course of study by . . .

3. I incorporated the following Design Qualities because . . .

4. The evidence of intellectual engagement that occurred during the implementation or is apparent in the work sample is . . .

5. When I analyzed the implementation of this lesson, and as I listened to your comments, I wondered if this lesson could be strengthened by . . .

These statements keep the session focused on the purpose at hand—examining student work to inform the teacher about his or her practice. They also prevent the presenting teacher from sounding defensive. Despite the fact that the statements are scripted, they require serious thought and can be answered only by teachers who are fully aware of the level of commitment a teacher makes when designing work for students. Presenting teachers can use Figure 5.4 to record notes on the various questions before the session begins and as the session progresses. This step should take approximately one third of the session time.

STEP 4: RAISING THE QUESTION

The last statement the presenting teacher completed in Step 3 detailed his or her thoughts about how the lesson could be strengthened. Now the same teacher asks his or her colleagues, "What else should I consider to strengthen this lesson?"

STEP 5: COLLEAGUES' RESPONSES TO THE QUESTION

In Step 5, the colleagues respond to the question posed in Step 4. Obviously, it is during this step that the words "trusted colleagues" are particularly valued. This trust can more easily be earned when the colleagues respond by focusing on lesson design, implementation, analysis, and reflection. Just as the presenting teacher's responses in Step 3 begin by completing statements, the colleagues' comments will be less threatening and more constructive if scripted also. Figure 5.5 is a Colleague Response Worksheet to help educators organize their thoughts. The following four gentle beginning lines will make suggestions effective but not disheartening:

- What are your thoughts on . . .
- What if you consider . . .
- It is evident . . .
- I found the following . . .

For example, one colleague might say, "What are your thoughts on defining the roles of individual students in group settings?" Or another colleague might suggest, "What if you consider selecting which students should be grouped together instead of allowing the students to form their own groups?" When the colleagues make these comments to the presenting teacher, he or she is not to respond. This is not a dialogue. These ideas are meant to be thought provoking, not to cause the presenting teacher to feel defensive. When the trusted colleagues are done sharing their thoughts, they should give their worksheets (Figure 5.5) to the presenting teacher. He or she can then refer to them during Step 6. Step 5 should take approximately one third of the time allotted. When this step is completed, the group members may leave.

STEP 6: REFLECTION

It is critical that the presenting teacher complete Step 6 after his or her colleagues depart the session. Taking the time for reflection on the entire session is vital to complete the process. These reflections should be recorded on the Discussion of Student Work Reflection Worksheet (Figure 5.6). The comments and suggestions of the trusted colleagues are to be thoughtfully considered during this reflective time. The reflections should be a balance of both the positive aspects and those areas that need adjustments. They should be based on the following questions:

- What have I learned about my practice through the discussion of these samples of student work? (Cover these areas: lesson design, implementation, analysis, and reflection.)
- What do I need to address in order to strengthen my practice?
- What area should become my priority?
- How am I going to address this area?
- Which student work samples should I include in my Professional Development Portfolio to chart my progress?

Ultimately, the consideration and use of the information and recommendations rests with the individual educator. Teachers participating in this process truly practice the standards of the profession. Well-intentioned comments from trusted colleagues are often thought provoking and helpful, but their ultimate impact depends on the presenting educator. He or she should consider whether any of the suggestions align with the documented findings in his or her Personal Teaching Inventory (see Chapter 4) and daily reflective journal (see Chapter 3). As patterns start to emerge they will become the basis of the educator's Professional Development Plan. (Refining the goals of the plan will be detailed in Chapter 6.) At this point, the presenting educator should select one of the student work samples to include in his or her professional development portfolio in order to have benchmarks of progress. The completed Reflection Worksheet should also become part of the portfolio entry. As subsequent examinations and discussions of student work are conducted, teachers should look for evidence of their growth in the areas they have chosen for professional development. Continued documentation of professional development will be evidenced in the professional development portfolio.

Often it is not only the presenting educator who reflects on the entire process. Although he or she reflects formally to inform his or her practice and to finalize and record the day's events, the other members of the collaborative learning team frequently reflect as well. Discussion of student work does not benefit one person alone. Everyone involved benefits from this experience.

Figure 5.7 is a sample of how one trusted colleague and one presenting teacher on a collaborative team completed the worksheets during a Guided Collaborative Discussion of Student Work session. The presenting teacher provided four samples of student work for the team to review and discuss. The samples were collected from her fifth-grade students as they worked on a unit of study on cultural heritage. All work samples had grading rubrics attached.

GUIDE FOR SUBSEQUENT DISCUSSIONS OF STUDENT WORK

As mentioned in the previous chapter, guided discussions of student work should be conducted at least once per month during the school year. When planning future discussion sessions, use the Guide for Subsequent Discussions of Student Work between Trusted Colleagues (Figure 5.8). Be certain to record upcoming discussion sessions on the calendar and do not merely have good intentions to conduct the next meeting. These dates can be agreed upon and added to the teachers' calendars at the start of the school year, which will honor all the participants and prove that everyone's work is valued (see Resource A). This also cements the fact that this is a group of trusted colleagues. Having one's student work examined by colleagues is not a step to be taken lightly. The benefits are too great to be erratic about scheduling sessions. Future sessions are also vital to the participants' Professional Development Plans. The Guided Collaborative Discussion of Student Work clearly illustrates the premise of the Collaborative Professional Development Process. It is a process that helps educators shift from the isolation of the closed classroom doors to powerful, rich collaboration with trusted colleagues.

Figure 5.1   Guide for the Collaborative Discussion of Student Work

- Each team meeting is evidence of personal commitment to the standards of the Collaborative Professional Development Process. It combines all the qualities that are stressed in this commitment. It is ongoing. It is reflective. It is collaborative.

- Using this process and the guiding questions that follow will help educators to truly examine the work they design for their students and ultimately will strengthen their practices.

- Select four students with a range of ability, two who are of similar ability, whose work will be examined throughout the school year.

Step 1: Presentation of Student Work

Without making comment, the presenting teacher shares samples of selected student work.

Step 2: Colleagues' Observations of Student Work

Trusted colleagues observe and comment on the work using the following guide:

- Infer nothing

- Describe the assignment in concrete terms, e.g., "This assignment was done individually. It is a report. Technology was used."

- Describe the evidence you see of Design Qualities

- Describe the evidence you see of Intellectual Engagement

Use the Observation Worksheet (Figure 5.2) to organize your thinking.

Step 3: Presenting Teacher's Response:

The presenting teacher completes the following five statements:

1. The purpose of this assignment was . . .

2. This assignment connects to the course of study by . . .

3. I incorporated the following Design Qualities because . . .

4. The evidence of intellectual engagement that occurred during the implementation or is apparent in the work samples is . . .

5. When I analyzed the implementation of this lesson, and as I listened to your comments, I wondered if this lesson could be strengthened by . . .

Step 4: Raising the Question

The presenting teacher asks the following question: What else should I consider to strengthen this lesson?

Step 5: Colleagues' Responses to the Question

The colleagues' responses should focus on lesson design, implementation, analysis, and reflection. Sentences that begin in the following manner tend to provide more constructive feedback:

- What are your thoughts on . . .

- What if you . . .

- It is evident . . .

- I found the following . . .

The presenting teacher listens and considers each suggestion without commenting.

Step 6: Reflection

The presenting teacher now sets aside time after the meeting to personally reflect on the session. He or she should think about the aspects of the session that were particularly powerful and pertinent to his or her practice. The teacher should reflect on both the positive aspects and those areas that need adjustment to ensure quality student learning. The reflections should be based on the following questions:

- What have I learned about my practice through the discussion of these samples of student work? (Cover these areas: lesson design, implementation, analysis, and reflection.)

- What do I need to address in order to strengthen my practice?

- What area should become my priority?

- How am I going to address this area?

- Which student work sample should I include in my professional development portfolio to chart my progress?

At this point, the presenting teacher will develop or revise his or her professional development plan.

Figure 5.2 Observation Worksheet

Record evidence in concrete terms. Please remember to infer nothing.

Describe the assignment.

_____

_____

_____

_____

Describe the evidence you see of Design Qualities.

_____

_____

_____

_____

Describe the evidence you see of Intellectual Engagement.

_____

_____

_____

_____

_____

Figure 5.3   Quick Reference Chart

Quick Reference Chart of the Design Qualities and Intellectual Engagement Indicators

Design Qualities	Intellectual Engagement Indicators
Product Focus	Persistence
Clear and Compelling Product Standards	Listening to Others With Understanding and Empathy
Protection From Adverse Consequences	Striving for Accuracy and Precision
Affirmation of Performance	Decreasing Impulsivity
Affiliation	Metacognition
Novelty and Variety	Cooperative Thinking
Choice	Reflection
Authenticity	Using All the Senses
Organization of Knowledge	Displaying a Sense of Humor
Content and Substance	Questioning and Problem Posing
	Drawing on Past Knowledge and Applying It to New Situations
	Ingenuity, Originality, Insight, Creativity
	Risk Taking
	Wonderment, Inquisitiveness, Curiosity, and the Enjoyment of Problem Solving

Figure 5.4   Presenting Teacher's Notes

The purpose of this assignment was

_____

_____

_____

This assignment connects to the course of study by

_____

_____

_____

I incorporated the following Design Qualities because

_____

_____

_____

_____

_____

The evidence of intellectual engagement that occurred during the implementation or is apparent in the work sample is

_____

_____

_____

_____

When I analyzed the implementation of this lesson, and as I listened to your comments, I wondered if this lesson could be strengthened by

_____

_____

_____

What else should I consider to strengthen this lesson? (Note colleagues' responses below)

_____

_____

_____

_____

_____

_____

Figure 5.5   Colleague Response Worksheet

What are your thoughts on

_____

_____

_____

What if you consider

_____

_____

_____

It is evident

_____

_____

_____

I found the following

_____

_____

_____

This worksheet is given to the presenting teacher at the end of the session. The presenting teacher can then use it for reference during Step 6: Reflection.

Figure 5.6 Discussion of Student Work Reflection Worksheet

These reflections should be a balance of both the positive aspects and those areas that need adjustments. They should be based on the following questions:

What have I learned about my practice through the discussion of these samples of student work? (Cover these areas: lesson design, implementation, analysis, and reflection.)

What do I need to address in order to strengthen my practice?

What area should become my priority?

How am I going to address this area?

_____

_____

_____

_____

_____

_____

_____

Which student work sample should I include in my professional development portfolio to chart my progress? _____

Figure 5.7   Sample Guided Collaborative Discussion Worksheets

Observation Worksheet

Record evidence in concrete terms. Please remember to infer nothing.

Describe the assignment.

This appears to be a Social Studies assignment dealing with different cultures. The student work samples are a picture accompanied by a report and rubric; a scroll with attached rubric; a scrapbook with descriptive captions and attached rubric; and a "cracker" with attached explanation, pictures, and rubric.

Describe the evidence you see of Design Qualities.

Product Focus: each work sample is a specific product relating to the student's heritage. *Novelty and Variety:* the work samples are varied in complexity and style. *Authenticity:* each work sample holds significant meaning for the student and connects with the child's real world. *Content and Substance:* the work is very much in line with the study of cultural heritage. *Choice:* due to the difference in work samples, it appears the students had some choice in the product they created.

Describe the evidence you see of Intellectual Engagement.

Striving for Accuracy and Precision: all the work samples appear to follow the attached rubrics. *Ingenuity, Originality, Insight, Creativity:* the work samples all appear to be creative, original work. *Wonderment, Inquisitiveness, Curiosity, and the Enjoyment of Problem Solving:* the students must have interviewed family members and consulted different resources to produce these finished work samples.

Presenting Teacher's Notes

The purpose of this assignment was

These work samples were collected as students completed the second of the following three goals: (1) Students will understand that the culture of a group includes its holidays, customs, language, beliefs, music, and food, and that much of a culture can be expressed through the arts; (2) Students will learn about their families' cultural heritages and those of their classmates through direct study and expression of these cultures through the arts; (3) Students will learn about the Chinese culture through a study of the Chinese New Year involving the arts.

This assignment connects to the course of study by

This unit logically followed the study of the ways natural resources and features identify a region in geography. This cultural heritage unit helps the learners explore how geography also includes the study of the way people live. The unit leads the students through a sequence built on their prior knowledge, starting with the familiar (their own cultural heritages) and progressing to the exploration of the unfamiliar (classmates' cultures and world, Chinese culture).

I incorporated the following Design Qualities because

Product Focus: I wanted the students' work to be connected with a cultural heritage project. *Choice:* I wanted the students to have ownership of their learning. *Authenticity:* I wanted the study of culture to be relevant to their lives. *Content and Substance:* I wanted the work produced by the students to come from the content, not just to be a fun add-on activity. *Affirmation of Performance:* I wanted the students to share their cultural heritages.

The evidence of intellectual engagement that occurred during the implementation or is apparent in the work sample

1. Ingenuity, Originality, Insight, Creativity
2. Striving for Accuracy and Precision
3. Listening to Others with Understanding and Empathy
4. Persistence
5. Metacognition
6. Questioning and Problem Posing

When I analyzed the implementation of this lesson, and as I listened to your comments, I wondered if this lesson could be strengthened by

Although I gave the students some choice in this assignment, they all were pretty safe in the ways they decided to present parts of their cultural heritages. I was really hoping to see a greater variety in the way that their information was presented. Perhaps this lesson could have been strengthened if I had encouraged more variety in the ways they presented their information.

What else should I consider to strengthen this lesson? (Note colleagues' responses below)

1. Evidence of some Design Qualities.
2. Work samples do not show a variety of the arts.
3. Evidence of a high level of intellectual engagement.
4. Many positive comments.

Colleague Response Worksheet

What are your thoughts on

the way the students presented their cultural heritage information? I thought all the work samples were well done. The students were able to work at their own abilities in the levels of complexity and ways that they chose to present their information. However, they all demonstrated that the students were knowledgeable about their heritages.

What if you consider

Your initial goals list the expression of the cultures through the arts. The visual arts are covered in these work samples. What if you had also encouraged the performing arts, music, and dance as ways to express their heritages?

(Continued)

Figure 5.7 (Continued)

It is evident

that the students enjoyed this assignment. The attention to detail in their work and the photographs show how they cared about what they were being asked to do, but at the same time they appeared to really be having a lot of fun.

I found the following

The work samples were based on many Design Qualities being embedded in the unit of study. The work samples display the fact that the students must have had a high level of intellectual engagement to produce work of this caliber.

This worksheet is given to the presenting teacher at the end of the session. The presenting teacher can then use it for reference during Step 6: Reflection.

Discussion of Student Work Reflection Worksheet

These reflections should be a balance of both the positive aspects and those areas that need adjustments. They should be based on the following questions:

What have I learned about my practice through the discussion of these samples of student work? (Cover these areas: lesson design, implementation, analysis, and reflection.)

What do I need to address in order to strengthen my practice?

What area should become my priority?

How am I going to address this area?

I was happy to see that my colleagues saw evidence of so many Design Qualities and Intellectual Engagement Indicators. I was also glad to see that my students' enthusiasm and excitement showed in the work samples and photographs.

I worked hard on my design of this unit and I think it showed. As I look back over my Unit Design Plan, I incorporated the introduction of the performing arts, music, and dance into some of the beginning activities so the students would have a sense of how they can define a culture. But now, as I reflect on my colleagues' remarks and look at the work samples again, I realize that the students did not use these art forms to tell about their cultural heritages. I think this may have to do with my implementation in the classroom when the students were deciding on the projects. I may have strongly encouraged the more traditional paper and pencil, tangible item projects that most of the students created. I think I need to address my implementation strategies in the classroom, particularly when individual or group projects are being decided on. I will start by watching this area in the remainder of this unit of study. I know this is also aligning with some of my daily reflective journal concerns. My implementation strategies need to become part of my Professional Development Plan.

Which student work sample should I include in my Professional Development Portfolio to chart my progress? Cultural heritage scrapbook

Figure 5.8   Guide for Subsequent Discussions of Student Work

Guide for Subsequent Discussions of Student Work between Trusted Colleagues

1. Discussions should be scheduled in advance, a minimum of once a month during the school year.

2. A time limit should be set at the beginning of each session.

3. Follow the "Guide for the Collaborative Discussion of Student Work" (Figure 5.1) to structure each session.

4. Discussions can be conducted in place of alternate staff meetings, as a regular focus of team meetings, or during professional development days.

5. Teachers note their reflections and findings from these meetings in their reflective journals (if their students' work was not shared) or in their professional growth portfolios (if they were the presenting educators).

6. At the end of the year, educators should consider what they have learned both personally and professionally as a result of this process and the impact it will have on their practices the following year.

6

Creating Professional Development Plans

A crucial part of the Collaborative Professional Development Process is the teachers' Professional Development Plans. Teachers begin to create their Professional Development Plans after the initial Guided Collaborative Discussion of their students' work and the subsequent Reflection. The plans are extremely personal and vital to the teachers' practices because they are based on the very work that the teachers have created for their students and analyzed with their trusted colleagues. This type of professional development is so effective because it stems from the work teachers design for their students, and its success is determined by the intellectual engagement and academic progress of those same students.

REFLECTION

Chapter 3 described the reflective thinking cycle. After the initial Guided Collaborative Discussion, the cycle begins with the presenting teacher reflecting on what he or she learned about his or her practice from the discussion of the student work samples (the Focus Stage). The power of the comments made by the teacher's trusted colleagues now lies with the presenting teacher. The teacher should focus on what has been learned about lesson design, implementation and analysis strategies, and reflective thinking practices. At this point, the teacher starts to recognize the areas that need to be addressed to strengthen his or her practice and ensure the intellectual engagement of the students. Reviewing the comments of the trusted colleagues and comparing those comments with their reflective journal and Personal Teaching Inventory will help teachers see the patterns that are beginning to emerge. This will help teachers to prioritize the areas they would like to strengthen and ultimately to choose the area that will be the focus of their Professional Development Plan.

Next the teacher asks questions to help clarify the focus selected for the Professional Development Plan (the Inquiry Stage). The following sample questions can be used to guide the teacher through this process. Over time, questions such as these will become automatic, and teachers will find that they are constantly questioning every aspect of their practices, leading to further growth at all stages of their careers.

Lesson Design Questions

- What evidence verifies that I know enough about the Design Qualities to adequately embed them in my lessons?
- Which of the Design Qualities are embedded in my lesson plans?
- What evidence verifies that I know enough about the Process Skills?
- How did I follow a lesson design template when creating my lesson plans, to ensure that the lesson evolves from specific Design Qualities with the intended Intellectual Engagement Indicators noted?
- How are my lessons inquiry based, with the students being the central, active participants in their own learning process?
- What evidence verifies that when planning my lessons I strategically plan student/teacher and student/student interactions so that my role (expert, facilitator, co-learner) as the teacher will vary throughout the lesson?

Implementation/Analysis Questions

- Do I have my lesson plans with me when I am with the class? Do I refer to them throughout the lesson to ensure that the strategies and outcomes that have been carefully planned are my focus during the lesson?
- How do I monitor my role during implementation and adjust it so that my students are taking an active part in their learning?
- What evidence shows that I can recognize the Intellectual Engagement Indicators during my implementation of the lessons?
- How do I watch for the planned Intellectual Engagement Indicators and adjust my role and the classroom atmosphere when they are absent or few in number?
- At the end of a lesson, how do I engage my students in a brief discussion of the Intellectual Engagement Indicators that they felt were present during the lesson?

- Does the evidence show that my lessons are carefully planned, but when implemented they lack the intellectual engagement of my students?

Reflection Questions

- What evidence do I have to illustrate that I am a reflective thinker?
- What reflective thinking model do I follow?
- Can I verbalize my basic educational beliefs?
- How do I document my reflective-strategic base?
- What steps am I currently taking to build a reflective thinking base in my practice?
- Do I keep a reflective journal?

The next step of the reflective thinking cycle is the Referencing Stage. The teacher cross-references the focus of his or her plan with previous Professional Development Plans (if any). If it is similar to past focuses, the teacher needs to refine this new focus to build on the growth that was accomplished with the previous Professional Development Plan. Reviewing the previous plan will help in the next step, when specific strategies are being developed. It is also important to recognize whether this is a new focus that the teacher has not spent time on previously. If it is an area of his or her practice that has never been given special attention, the development of it may require an extended amount of time. With this realization, the teacher will be less likely to become discouraged if growth is not seen immediately, but rather develops over a period of time.

WRITING THE PROFESSIONAL DEVELOPMENT PLAN

Teachers write their Professional Development Plans during the Strategy Stage of the reflective thinking cycle. The plan should describe the specific strategies that the teacher intends to use to address the focus area. Figure 6.1 is a Professional Development Plan template that teachers may find helpful. In addition, Chapters 7 through 9 will give teachers a starting point for the development of their focus area strategies; each of these chapters covers one of the professional development focus areas. Additional readings can also be found in the Bibliography. The development of the Professional Development Plan is very personal. Although the teacher has analyzed his or her practice with trusted colleagues during the Guided Collaborative Discussion of Student Work sessions, the professional development strategy ultimately rests with the individual teacher. It is during the last stage of the reflective cycle that the teacher synthesizes all the information concerning his or her practice and draws up a plan that is highly personal and specific.

Figure 6.1   Professional Development Plan Template

Focus for Professional Development:

Lesson Design   ____

Lesson Implementation   ____

Lesson Analysis   ____

Reflective Practice   ____

Focus for my own learning:

_____

_____

_____

Specific strategies I will implement to address this Focus:

_____

_____

_____

Evidence of Success: Description of student work samples and dates they were added to professional portfolio. (The number of samples collected will depend on the length of time required to complete this focus.)

Sample One: _____Date_____

Sample Two: _____Date_____

Sample Three: _____Date_____

Sample Four: _____Date_____

Sample Five: _____Date_____

Sample Six: _____Date_____

Date this focus has been strengthened sufficiently that a new focus needs to be identified for my professional growth: _____

This Professional Development Plan should be included in your professional development portfolio.

Many school districts require that teachers have a Professional Development Plan in place at the beginning of the school year. Teachers who intend to use the Collaborative Professional Development Process to guide their professional development could simply state that on their plans at the beginning of the year. They can state that they are going to incorporate the collaborative process into their practices to further shape and refine their professional development goals.

FURTHER STUDY TO GUIDE PROFESSIONAL DEVELOPMENT

After the Professional Development Plan has been written, teachers begin to implement their professional development strategies. Due to the unique design of the Collaborative Professional Development Process, professional development concentrates on lesson design (Chapter 7), lesson implementation strategies (Chapter 8), lesson analysis during instruction (Chapter 9), and reflective practices (Chapter 3). Each of these is a professional development focus area in the Collaborative Professional Development Process. Over time, as teachers study and strengthen these professional development areas, their overall practice is strengthened as well. As new work is designed and implemented in the classroom, teachers pay close attention to their professional development focus areas.

SUBSEQUENT COLLABORATIVE DISCUSSIONS OF STUDENT WORK

In subsequent discussions of student work, the professional development focus becomes highly important as the presenting teacher looks for evidence indicating professional growth has taken place in the focus area. Student work samples that illustrate this growth are then added to the teacher's professional development portfolio.

After each session and the reflection that follows, the Professional Development Plan can be adjusted as the teacher's practice becomes stronger and successful teaching strategies become part of his or her teaching repertoire. It is during this reflective time that teachers determine whether they have adequately met their professional development goals. It is important that these reflections are based on the evidence that has been presented, and acknowledged by their trusted colleagues, in their student work samples.

As professional development goals are accomplished, new goals are set and teachers study new focus areas, thus continuing to refine and improve their practices. The Collaborative Professional Development Process is cyclic in that teachers constantly evaluate their practices by examining student work and designing their own continuing professional development (see Chapter 1, Figure 1.1).

Professional development that stems from teachers becoming part of learning communities with trusted colleagues is perhaps the highest form of professional development. These communities empower teachers to personally transform their practices and deepen their professional commitments. The National Board for Professional Teaching Standards (1991) believes in the strength of learning communities. The National Board standard number five—"Teachers are members of learning communities"— recognizes the strength that collegial interaction with peers brings to a teacher's practice. When teachers engage in professional development of this caliber, they in fact become the ultimate role models for their students. They serve as evidence of their own teaching philosophy: that the goal of education should be for children and adults to become lifelong learners, constantly striving to assess their progress and deepen their learning.

7

Designing Quality Lessons

Up to this point, educators completing the Collaborative Professional Development Process have thoroughly read and reflected on the standards upon which this plan is based. They have assessed themselves and determined the areas they excel in and those that they wish to strengthen. They have experienced the Guided Collaborative Discussion of Student Work process. They have seen the correlation between the lesson Design Qualities and the Intellectual Engagement Indicators.

No one would pursue the Collaborative Professional Development endeavor without intending to improve his or her practice. As educators complete the steps of the process, areas of their practice that need attention naturally emerge. The Collaborative Professional Development Process is designed so that the practice areas can be grouped into one of the following four categories: lesson design, lesson implementation strategies, lesson analysis during instruction, and reflection. Chapters 7 through 9 are devoted to these vital areas. By strengthening their practice in these areas, educators will accomplish their professional development goals. This chapter discusses the first of the four categories, lesson design.

Designing units and lessons is a professional development area that many teachers want to investigate and address. Planning is such a basic element of a teacher's practice that erroneously it could be assumed all teachers accomplish it with ease. On the contrary, teachers commonly identify it as an area needing improvement. Despite completing recommended formats for lesson plans and addressing the course of study, teachers are sometimes unable to produce evidence that the plans they create result in the anticipated student understanding and student work.

Hallmarks of ineffective unit and lesson design can cover a large range of behaviors. On one hand, there are overburdened teachers planning work in an inefficient, "one more thing to do" manner, instead of thoughtfully, with long-range goals in mind. Too often one hears teachers lamenting that it is the end of the week and their lesson plans have not yet been started. Whether it is a matter of not knowing any better, or simply a matter of feeling unimaginative, the concern is real. Work that is designed for students should not be an afterthought at the end of a busy week. It should not be a late-night Sunday albatross around one's neck. Nor should it be a series of isolated lessons that are planned in a disjointed, disconnected manner.

At the other end of the lesson design focus group, there are the educators who already do much more. They select performance indicators and objectives that link with the course of study. They have an understanding and mastery of what they must teach and have an enthusiasm for doing so in the best ways possible. But even these teachers find themselves focusing on the logistics of covering ever-increasing requirements in the school year. This can result in concentration on the requirements rather than on mastery by the students. How can student comprehension and coverage of material be successfully meshed in the planning stages? As discussed in Chapter 2, this can be accomplished by designing lessons that incorporate Design Qualities and indicating in the lesson plan the Intellectual Engagement Indicators that should be visible when the lessons are taught. In order to accomplish this in an organized manner, it is crucial that educators follow a unit design format that requires careful thought, not only about the curriculum content, but about the higher-level thinking processes as well.

THE UNDERSTANDING BY DESIGN MODEL

Wiggins and McTighe (1998) have developed one of the most highly regarded unit design models. Their unit design theory promotes teaching for understanding, meaning that "a student has something more than just textbook knowledge and skill—that a students really 'gets it.' Understanding, then, involves sophisticated insights and abilities, reflected in varied performances and contexts" (p. 5). This particular unit design theory correlates well with the Collaborative Professional Development Process and the research of Schlechty (1997) and Costa and Liebmann (1997a). The work of Wiggins and McTighe, Schlechty, Costa and Liebmann, and the Collaborative Professional Development Process can be blended together into a powerful unit design process. Wiggins and McTighe "describe the most effective curricular designs as backward" (p. 8). Their unit design system is a three-stage planning sequence.

Stage One

In the first stage, the teacher identifies the results that students should achieve by the end of the unit. Teachers must consider goals, content standards, and the required curriculum. It is suggested that teachers prioritize concepts as "worth being familiar with," "important knowledge and skills," or "enduring understandings" (pp. 9-10). Enduring understandings are highly regarded beliefs held by experts in the field of study. These understandings have endured over time and are of considerable value to educated people. Enduring understandings are the concepts that students will retain long after the unit is complete.

Prioritizing Concepts

Wiggins and McTighe (1998) offer four "filters" or questions to help teachers prioritize lesson concepts. These filters correlate with Schlechty's (1997) Design Qualities:

- *Filter 1*: To what extent does the idea, topic, or process represent a "big idea" having enduring value beyond the classroom? (Corresponds to the Design Quality "Authenticity")
- *Filter 2*: To what extent does the idea, topic, or process reside at the heart of the discipline? (Corresponds to the Design Qualities "Content and Substance" and "Organization of Knowledge")
- *Filter 3*: To what extent does the idea, topic, or process require "uncoverage of the material—inquiring into, around, and underneath content instead of simply covering it"? (p. 98; Corresponds to the Design Quality "Content and Substance")
- *Filter 4*: To what extent does the idea, topic, or process offer potential for engaging students? (Corresponds to the Design Qualities "Product Focus," "Affiliation," "Novelty and Variety," "Choice," and "Affirmation of Performance")

There are many topics related to the required curriculum content that are of value and interest, but, realistically, not everything can be thoroughly presented. The filters help teachers prioritize what can and should be covered in the time they have available.

Facets of Understanding

Wiggins and McTighe (1998) believe there is a difference between students "knowing" and students "understanding," and they divide understanding into six different facets. These facets align with Costa and Liebmann's (1997a) Intellectual Engagement Indicators. Wiggins and McTighe believe that all units of study should be viewed through these six facets. When activities and strategies are developed around the Design Qualities, students who truly understand will be able to demonstrate their understanding via the following:

- *Facet 1*: Explanation (Corresponds to the Intellectual Engagement Indicators "Questioning and Problem Posing," "Persistence," "Decreasing Impulsivity," and "Wonderment, Inquisitiveness, Curiosity, and the Enjoyment of Problem Solving")
- *Facet 2*: Interpretation (Corresponds to the Intellectual Engagement Indicators "Questioning and Problem Posing," "Metacognition," "Using All the Senses," and "Reflection")
- *Facet 3*: Application (Corresponds to the Intellectual Engagement Indicators "Drawing on Past Knowledge and Applying It to New Situations" and "Reflection")
- *Facet 4*: Perspective (Corresponds to the Intellectual Engagement Indicators "Ingenuity, Originality, Insight, Creativity," "Listening to Others With Understanding and Empathy," "Cooperative Thinking," and "Displaying a Sense of Humor")
- *Facet 5*: Empathy (Corresponds to the Intellectual Engagement Indicator "Listening to Others with Understanding and Empathy")
- *Facet 6*: Self-knowledge (Corresponds to the Intellectual Engagement Indicators "Metacognition" and "Reflection")

As teachers design units of study around these six facets, they will see how various Intellectual Engagement Indicators naturally align with the facets. The alignments indicated above are only meant to be a starting point for teachers to develop their own understanding of the correlations between the two.

When planning units of study with the six facets of understanding in mind, teachers can identify the "enduring understanding" to be developed during the unit by considering the essential concepts they want the students to understand by the completion of the unit. The understandings need to be phrased in generalizations that begin with the words, "Students will understand that . . . ." Teachers should use their content standards to guide the development of the enduring understanding. Next, teachers should develop essential questions that will steer their teaching and encourage student inquiry. The essential questions have no obvious correct answer. They are debatable and worth debating, and they keep arising in discussions. They raise other important queries and lead to related issues in the discipline being studied. They help students focus on their final performances.

Stage Two

In stage two, teachers thoughtfully develop assessments that will provide evidence of students' understanding. Assessments should be based on the six facets and the corresponding Intellectual Engagement Indicators. These assessments should range from informal checks for understanding to observations and discussions, tests and quizzes, academic prompts, and performance tasks and projects. The assessments also should be aligned with the Design Qualities "Clear and Compelling

Product Standards" and "Protection From Adverse Consequences." Using a variety of assessments will provide a two-fold result: it will offer a balanced approach to an overall unit; and it will provide opportunities throughout the unit to promote and monitor learning, rather than merely measuring it on completion.

Stage Three

Stage three of the process is the planning of learning experiences and instruction. This is not writing detailed lesson plans but is an outline of the main lessons and activities that the students will experience. Wiggins and McTighe (1998) coined the term "uncoverage." Teachers should design units that require students to produce evidence that demonstrates their understanding. The facets of understanding and corresponding Intellectual Engagement Indicators demand that students explain, interpret, and apply. They must demonstrate perspective, empathy, and self-knowledge. To accomplish this, teachers must design lessons that require the students to use the facets in order to encounter the lesson content. Lessons that are rich in the Design Qualities do just that. They encourage inquiry-based instruction where students pursue the content in depth and with breadth. Despite all the things that textbooks do well with respect to information, organization, and consideration of their audience, they are notorious for reducing concepts to succinct summaries and simplistic endings. That is why the textbook should be one source and not the sole basis for designing and planning work for students. Students need to have opportunities to delve into material through other means. Connection to other experiences, statistics, and concepts will give breadth to students' understanding. Teachers need to plan opportunities for creating specific yet simple models of the concepts being uncovered. They need to represent the ideas in various ways and provide opportunities for students to go past the original concept and imagine other possibilities. With these efforts, stage three prompts the teachers to select experiences and strategies that will result in the desired understandings, enthusiastic involvement, and greater probability of a high level of performance by their students. The evidence will be the high level of intellectual engagement displayed by the students.

LESSON DESIGN RESOURCES

Educators may find it daunting at first to embed the Design Qualities into their unit designs and link them with the anticipated Intellectual Engagement Indicators. For this reason, Figure 7.1 can be used as a beginning reference point. As teachers become more familiar with the work of Schlechty and Costa and Liebmann, they will be able to make new connections on their own based on their unique unit designs.

(Text continues on page 85)

Figure 7.1   Intellectual Engagement Indicators and Corresponding Design
Qualities

As discussed throughout this book, there is detectable evidence when students
display intellectually engaged behaviors. The indicators of these behaviors are
explained in detail in the Table below. Units of study and individual lessons
should be carefully planned so these indicators can be taught and encouraged
on a daily basis. When they are embedded in the lessons and students practice
them daily, they become habits that students can employ as they become
lifelong learners.

Educators can use this document to carefully plan, implement, and analyze
their lessons. The Design Qualities that educators need to embed in their lessons
to achieve the intellectual engagement of their students are indicated as well. It
is vital that educators skillfully plan for and direct the engagement of their
students and not leave it to chance.

Intellectual Engagement Indicators	Corresponding Design Qualities
1. Cooperative Thinking	
Together people are more powerful (i.e., intellectually, physically) than any one person alone	
A. Individual actions of a group participant (i.e., open to feedback, willingness to use others' ideas, contribute and justify ideas of others)	• Protection From Adverse Consequences for Initial Failure • Affirmation of Performance • Affiliation
B. Group dynamics (i.e., actively listen, seek consensus and support group efforts, display empathy, sensitivity to the needs of others, compassion)	• Protection From Adverse Consequences for Initial Failure • Affiliation • Authenticity
2. Ingenuity, Originality, Insight, Creativity	
Creative people often conceive problem solutions differently, examining alternative possibilities. They constantly strive for fluency, elaboration, novelty, simplicity, competence, perfection, beauty, harmony, and balance.	
A. Take risks and push the boundaries of their perceived limits	• Protection From Adverse Consequences for Initial Failure
B. Motivated intrinsically	

(Continued)

Figure 7.1 (Continued)

Intellectual Engagement Indicators	Corresponding Design Qualities
C. Open to criticism	• Protection From Adverse Consequences for Initial Failure • Affirmation of Performance
D. Examine status quo	• Protection From Adverse Consequences for Initial Failure
E. Generate original, clever, and ingenious products, solutions, and techniques	• Protection From Adverse Consequences for Initial Failure • Novelty and Variety • Choice
F. Project themselves into different roles using analogies	• Novelty and Variety • Choice
G. Exhibit products for judgment and feedback in an effort to refine process and product	• Clear and Compelling Product Standards • Protection From Adverse Consequences for Initial Failure • Affirmation of Performance
3. Listening to Others With Understanding and Empathy	
A. Recognize others' feelings or emotional state (i.e., detect verbal cues and body language)	• Affiliation
B. Accurately express another person's concepts, emotions, and problems (i.e., paraphrase, build on the ideas and feelings, clarify, give examples)	• Clear and Compelling Product Standards • Protection From Adverse Consequences for Initial Failure • Affiliation
4. Metacognition: Awareness of our own thinking	
Metacognition means becoming increasingly aware of one's actions and their effect on others and the environment, forming internal questions, developing mental maps or plans of action, mentally rehearsing prior to performance, and monitoring plans as they are employed.	
A. Verbalize essential questions when presented with new learning such as: Whose perspective? What is the evidence? What are the connections to previous learning? What is the relevance of this problem? What inferences can be made?	• Clear and Compelling Product Standards • Novelty and Variety • Organization of Knowledge

Intellectual Engagement Indicators	Corresponding Design Qualities
B. Clarify and understand directions	• Product Focus • Clear and Compelling Product Standards
C. Develop a plan of action	
D. Withhold immediate value judgments	• Novelty and Variety
E. Develop and describe the strategies, steps, and sequences in the problem-solving process	• Product Focus • Choice
F. Intentionally form a vision of a product, plan of action, goal, or destination before beginning	• Product Focus • Clear and Compelling Product Standards • Choice
G. Implement the plan of action	
5. Reflection	
A. Through reflection determine if a plan is working or needs to be changed while in progress	
i. Analyze the data	• Clear and Compelling Product Standards • Novelty and Variety
ii. Make changes if the plan is not meeting expectations	• Clear and Compelling Product Standards • Protection From Adverse Consequences for Initial Failure
B. Reflection upon completion	
i. Review the plan, processes, and products	• Clear and Compelling Product Standards
ii. Edit mental pictures for improved future performance	• Clear and Compelling Product Standards
C. Reflective people also consider and evaluate the quality of their own thinking skills and strategies.	
i. Learners self-reflect to enhance personal growth	
ii. Evaluate performance	• Clear and Compelling Product Standards
iii. Evaluate thought processes	• Clear and Compelling Product Standards
6. Persistence: Sticking to a task when a solution is not apparent.	

(Continued)

Figure 7.1 (Continued)

Intellectual Engagement Indicators	Corresponding Design Qualities
A. Consider a variety of strategies	• Product Focus • Clear and Compelling Product Standards • Novelty and Variety • Choice
B. Select a strategy, implement, collect evidence	• Product Focus • Clear and Compelling Product Standards • Protection From Adverse Consequences for Initial Failure • Novelty and Variety • Choice • Organization of Knowledge
C. Try alternative strategies, as needed	• Product Focus • Clear and Compelling Product Standards • Protection From Adverse Consequences for Initial Failure • Novelty and Variety • Choice
7. Questioning and Problem Posing	
A. Formulate questions to fill in the gaps between the known and unknown	• Product Focus • Clear and Compelling Product Standards
B. Ask a variety and range of questions (i.e., requests for date, what-ifs)	• Novelty and Variety
C. Recognize discrepancies	• Organization of Knowledge
D. Probe causes	• Novelty and Variety • Content and Substance
E. Investigate ideas	• Novelty and Variety • Choice • Content and Substance
8. Drawing on Past Knowledge and Applying It to New Situations	
A. Draw on stored knowledge and past experiences to solve new challenges	• Novelty and Variety • Organization of Knowledge
B. Connect new knowledge and make immediate and meaningful application	• Product Focus • Authenticity • Content and Substance
9. Displaying a Sense of Humor	
A. Employ creative approaches to thinking	

Intellectual Engagement Indicators	Corresponding Design Qualities
B. Find incongruities and discontinuities	• Novelty and Variety • Organization of Knowledge
C. Perceive absurdities, ironies, or satire	• Novelty and Variety • Organization of Knowledge
D. Distinguish when situations are appropriate for laughter	• Novelty and Variety • Content and Substance
E. Distinguish between human frailty and fallibilities that are in need of compassion and those situations that are truly funny	
10. Striving for Accuracy and Precision	
A. Take time to check over processes and products throughout	
i. Review the rules (procedures)	• Clear and Compelling Product Standards
ii. Review the criteria (product standards)	• Product Focus • Clear and Compelling Product Standards
iii. Review the models and vision	• Product Focus • Clear and Compelling Product Standards
iv. Evaluate and modify work as needed	• Clear and Compelling Product Standards • Protection From Adverse Consequences
v. Confirm finished product meets criteria	• Product Focus • Clear and Compelling Product Standards • Affirmation of Performance
B. Communicate accurately in both written and oral forms	
i. Use correct names, universal labels, and analogies	• Authenticity • Organization of Knowledge • Content and Substance
ii. Define, clarify, and elaborate on the terminology	• Authenticity • Organization of Knowledge • Content and Substance

(Continued)

Figure 7.1 (Continued)

Intellectual Engagement Indicators	Corresponding Design Qualities
iii. Develop criteria spontaneously for their own value judgments and explain their rationale	• Product Focus • Clear and Compelling Product Standards • Novelty and Variety
11. Using All the Senses: Sensory pathways that are open, alert, and acute can absorb more information.	
A. Use all the senses to explore and absorb	• Novelty and Variety
B. Conceive and express many ways to solve problems by using the senses (i.e., make observations, gather data, experiment, role play, simulate, manipulate, scrutinize, identify variables, interview, break problems into components, visualize, imitate, illustrate, and build models)	• Novelty and Variety • Choice • Authenticity
12. Wonderment, Inquisitiveness, Curiosity and the Enjoyment of Problem Solving	
A. Enjoy problem solving	
i. Seek out existing problems	• Novelty and Variety • Choice
ii. Make up original problems	• Novelty and Variety • Choice
B. Acutely aware of their surroundings	
i. Reflect on changes in the surroundings	• Novelty and Variety • Authenticity
ii. Appreciate intricacies of nature (i.e., cloud formations, spider webs)	• Novelty and Variety • Authenticity
iii. Understand their role as part of a larger community and universe	• Affirmation of Performance • Affiliation • Authenticity

Intellectual Engagement Indicators	Corresponding Design Qualities
13. Decreasing Impulsivity: Managing impulsivity means to refrain from acting or reacting immediately	
A. Taking the time to think before acting or speaking	• Product Focus • Clear and Compelling Product Standards
B. Refraining from interrupting and truly listening as others are expressing ideas, emotions, opinions	• Affiliation
C. Thoroughly thinking through an idea before responding	• Organization of Knowledge • Content and Substance
D. Understanding and appreciating the rewards of delayed gratification	• Authenticity
E. Taking the time to employ other habits of the mind when solving problems	• Choice
14. Risk Taking: Risk takers are uncomfortable with comfort. They are compelled to go beyond the established limits.	
A. Live on the edge of their competence level	• Novelty and Variety • Choice
B. View setbacks as challenging and growth producing	

Figure 7.2 is a Unit Design Plan template that teachers can use to plan units of study. It will help teachers pay particular attention to embedding the Design Qualities throughout the unit, along with the corresponding Intellectual Engagement Indicators that should be evidenced during the implementation of the unit. It will guide teachers in the planning of lessons in a thorough and thoughtful manner. Teachers may use it as it appears or they may want to create a form of their own. The important thing to remember is that highly effective teachers follow a definite, thoughtful plan of action when designing the work they ask their students to complete.

Figure 7.3 is a completed Unit Design Plan. It was completed by a fourth-grade teacher for a unit of study in science. Reviewing this Unit Design Plan will help educators see how the key elements of current research can be smoothly blended together to produce powerful results in student learning.

Figure 7.2   Unit Design Plan

Unit of Study: _____

Date Created: _____

Broad Unit Objectives	Student Understandings

Evidence of Student Learning

Anticipated Intellectual Engagement Indicators for Student Tasks and
Investigations

Student Tasks and Investigations	Corresponding Design Qualities	Anticipated Intellectual Engagement Indicators

Evidence of Student Learning

Anticipated Intellectual Engagement Indicators for Investigative Group
Participation, Work Samples, Class Participation

Investigative Group Participation, Work Samples, Class Participation	Corresponding Design Qualities	Anticipated Intellectual Engagement Indicators

(Continued)

Figure 7.2 (Continued)

Evidence of Student Acquisition of Unit Objectives

Content-Specific

Evidence of Student Acquisition of Unit Objectives

Student Self-Assessment

| |
| |
| |
| |
| |
| |
| |
| |
| |
| |
| |
| |
| |

(Continued)

Figure 7.2 (Continued)

Classroom Experiences

(Where lessons built on the Design Qualities will Intellectually
Engage the students)

Experiences	Corresponding Design Qualities

Reflections

(To be completed following the implementation of this unit of study)

Based on the evidence, was this unit of study successfully implemented? (Reflection should document the Intellectual Engagement Indicators that were witnessed in the classroom.)

Were there powerful events that happened spontaneously that provided additional evidence of student intellectual engagement and understanding? (Reflection should document the events and corresponding Intellectual Engagement Indicators.)

(Continued)

Figure 7.2 (Continued)

Based on the above reflections, was this unit of study successfully implemented and did it result in the desired student intellectual engagement and understanding?

If this unit of study was not successful and did not result in the desired evidence of student understanding, reflect on the lesson implementation and daily analysis as the unit was taught. Further study of lesson implementation or analysis may be needed. (Refer to Chapters 8 and 9.)

If the reflective section of this plan was difficult for you to complete, refer to Chapter 3.

Figure 7.3   Sample Unit Design Plan

Unit Design Plan

Unit of Study: <u>States of Matter–Physical and Chemical Changes in Matter</u>

Date Created: _____

Broad Unit Objectives	Student Understandings
The students will understand:	
Elements of a physical change in matter	Students will understand that a physical change in matter
• Change in state of matter	• changes the state of the matter such as melting, evaporation, freezing, and condensation
	• can also change size and shape of matter
	• does not form new matter
Elements of a chemical change in matter	Students will understand that a chemical change in matter
• Forms new kind of matter	• forms new kinds of matter
	• involves energy

(Continued)

Figure 7.3 (Continued)

Evidence of Student Learning

Anticipated Intellectual Engagement Indicators for Student Tasks and Investigations

Student Tasks and Investigations	Corresponding Design Qualities	Anticipated Intellectual Engagement Indicators
1. Creation of "Know, Want to Know, New Knowledge" chart.	1. Organization of Knowledge; Content and Substance	1. Drawing on Past Knowledge and Applying to New Situations
2. Investigations centered around exploring melting point, evaporation, boiling point, condensation, and freezing point.	2. Affiliation; Choice; Organization of Knowledge	2. Cooperative Thinking; Ingenuity, Originality, Insight; Persistence; Questioning and Problem Posing; Decreasing Impulsivity
3. Charting freezing or melting times of common food items.	3. Organization of Knowledge; Authenticity; Choice	3. Persistence; Striving for Accuracy and Precision; Risk Taking
4. Investigation: add aluminum foil plus copper sulfate, salt, and water. Forms tangible new matter (copper).	4. Affiliation; Organization of Knowledge	4. Cooperative Thinking; Listening to Others; Metacognition
5. Investigation: add baking soda to vinegar to create new matter (gas). Bubbles indicate energy.	5. Affiliation	5. Cooperative Thinking
6. Recording findings in Scientific Journals (write, draw, diagram, etc., student choice).	6. Organization of Knowledge; Protection from Adverse Consequences	6. Striving for Accuracy & Precision; Persistence
7. Group projects demonstrating or illustrating physical and chemical changes.	7. Novelty and Variety; Product Focus; Affiliation; Authenticity; Choice	7. Using All the Senses; Persistence; Listening to Others; Cooperative Thinking; Metacognition
8. Student self-assessing and assessing peer projects.	8. Clear and Compelling Product Standards	8. Metacognition
9. Sharing projects with other classes	9. Affirmation of Performance	9. Ingenuity, Originality, Insight

Evidence of Student Learning

Anticipated Intellectual Engagement Indicators for Investigative Group
Participation, Work Samples, Class Participation

Investigative Group Participation, Work Samples, Class Participation	Corresponding Design Qualities	Anticipated Intellectual Engagement Indicators
1. Observations during investigations.	1. Affiliation; Choice; Organization of Knowledge	1. Cooperative Thinking; Listening to Others; Ingenuity, Originality, Insight; Persistence; Questioning and Problem Posing; Decreasing Impulsivity; Metacognition
2. Work samples charting freezing and melting times of common foods.	2. Organization of Knowledge; Authenticity; Choice	2. Persistence; Striving for Accuracy and Precision; Risk Taking
3. Scientific Journals	3. Organization of Knowledge; Protection From Adverse Consequences	3. Striving for Accuracy and Precision; Persistence
4. Group Projects	4. Novelty and Variety; Product Focus; Affiliation; Authenticity; Choice	4. Using All the Senses; Persistence; Listening to Others With Understanding; Cooperative Thinking; Metacognition
5. Student self-assessing and assessing peer projects and Rubrics	5. Clear and Compelling; Product Standards	5. Metacognition; Reflection; Striving for Accuracy and Precision
6. Daily discussions on anticipated and witnessed Intellectual Engagement.	6. Protection From Adverse Consequences	6. Reflection; Metacognition
7. Sharing projects with other classes.	7. Affirmation of Performance	7. Ingenuity, Originality, Insight and Creativity

(Continued)

Figure 7.3 (Continued)

Evidence of Student Acquisition of Unit Objectives

Content-Specific

Quiz 1: Physical changes in matter.
Quiz 2: Chemical changes in matter.
Prompt: Describe a physical and a chemical change in matter. Stress what is needed for a chemical change that is not necessary for a physical change to take place.

Evidence of Student Acquisition of Unit Objectives

Student Self-Assessment

1. Students will self-assess their participation in the group projects.
2. Students will self-assess the group projects.
3. Students will self-assess their charts on the freezing or melting times of common food items.
4. Students will self-assess their journal entries on physical and chemical changes in matter.
5. Students will self-assess their intellectual engagement daily.
*Students will use student created rubrics and personal reflective journals.

Classroom Experiences

(Where lessons built on the Design Qualities will Intellectually Engage the students)

Experiences	Corresponding Design Qualities
1. Together create "Know, Want to Know, New Knowledge" chart centered on physical and chemical changes in matter.	1. Organization of Knowledge; Content and Substance
2. Introduce broad unit objectives.	2. Content and Substance
3. Student teams conduct student-designed investigations centered on melting point, evaporation, boiling point, condensation, and freezing point (physical changes in matter).	3. Affiliation; Choice; Organization of Knowledge
4. Chart freezing or melting times of common food items.	4. Organization of Knowledge; Authenticity; Choice
5. Student teams investigate the combining of copper sulfate, salt, and water solutions with aluminum foil resulting in new matter (copper).	5. Affiliation; Organization of Knowledge
6. Student teams will investigate adding baking soda to vinegar creating new matter (gas).	6. Affiliation
7. Students record findings in their Scientific Journals (write, draw, diagram, etc., student choice).	7. Organization of Knowledge; Choice
8. Teacher feedback on participation in teams. Scientific Journals and team projects.	8. Protection From Adverse Consequences
9. Daily concluding discussions on Intellectual Engagement that took place that day.	9. Protection From Adverse Consequences
10. Students design group projects to demonstrate chemical and physical changes in matter.	10. Novelty and Variety; Product Focus; Affiliation; Authenticity; Choice
11. Students self-assess and assess their peers.	11. Clear and Compelling Product Standards
12. Sharing projects with other classes.	12. Affirmation of Performance

(Continued)

Figure 7.3 (Continued)

Reflections

(To be completed following the implementation of this unit of study)

Based on the evidence, was this unit of study successfully implemented? (Reflection should document the Intellectual Engagement Indicators that were witnessed in the classroom.)

> This unit of study was highly successful. During the investigations and group projects, the students demonstrated all of the anticipated Intellectual Engagement Indicators. The students' individual Scientific Journals confirmed that 94 percent of the class understood the chemical and physical changes in matter. After conferencing and one-on-one work with several students, this rose to 100 percent. The two paper-and-pencil quizzes also verified that all the students understood the material covered. This unit of study gave the students the ability to work independently and with their peers. As I reflect on their work, I wonder if this unit couldn't be strengthened by bringing more community members in to share how understanding the changes in matter is vital to the adult work they are doing daily? This would certainly help to make this unit more relevant to the students' lives. I also wonder if I could pair the students differently to help them achieve more depth in the investigations they conducted?

Were there powerful events that happened spontaneously that provided additional evidence of student intellectual engagement and understanding? (Reflection should document the events and corresponding Intellectual Engagement Indicators.)

> 1. After investigating with the baking soda and vinegar one student team wanted to stretch a balloon across the opening of the jar their mixture was in. The gas in the jar inflated the balloon, illustrating that a chemical change can bring about a physical change (in the balloon) as well. Intellectual Engagement Indicators: Risk Taking, Questioning & Problem Solving, Wonderment, Inquisitiveness, Curiosity & the Enjoyment of Problem Solving.

> 2. Students helping other peer teams to adjust their investigations to bring about success. Intellectual Engagement Indicators: Cooperative Thinking, Striving for Accuracy & Precision, Persistence, Listening to Others With Understanding and Empathy.

> 3. Students wanting to invite a chemical engineer to the class to discuss changes in matter and his or her profession. This was arranged and was very successful. Intellectual Engagement Indicators: Wonderment, Inquisitiveness, Curiosity, and the Enjoyment of Problem Solving; Reflection

Based on the above reflections, was this unit of study successfully implemented, and did it result in the desired student intellectual engagement and understanding?

Yes

If this unit of study was not successful, and did not result in the desired evidence of student understanding, reflect on the implementation and daily analysis as the unit was taught. Further study of lesson implementation or analysis may be needed. (Refer to Chapters 8 and 9.)

If the reflective section of this plan was difficult for you to complete, refer to Chapter 3.

8

Exploring Instructional Strategies

This chapter will look closely at implementing lessons that incorporate Design Qualities. These lessons have been designed to foster independent thinking in which learning is self-directed and intellectual engagement is a predictable result (see also Chapter 2). However, even the best-laid lesson plans can fall short of their intended outcomes if the teachers who created them do not implement the lessons with care. Teachers must be diligent in their implementation of quality lessons, so that their personal behaviors and the classroom community encourage the students to be active participants in their learning experience. These are classrooms in which students are excited about learning, and the teachers and students work together toward a common goal. It is here, in front of the students in the classroom, that teachers' quality lesson plans can elevate their students to new learning horizons that reach far beyond the physical boundaries of the classroom walls. With poor implementation, the same plans can reduce the students to mere passive receivers of the required content knowledge.

THE CHANGING ROLE OF THE TEACHER

Like teachers of years ago, many teachers today act as though they are on stage performing for their students. Many educators feel that they have to compete with high-energy action-packed video games, television, movies, and music video personalities in order to capture the attention of their students. They treat their students as passive, unresponsive vessels that they must entertain and educate at the same time. They feel their effectiveness as educators depends on how well they entertain and control the students' every move and even their thinking. This "Sage on Stage" scenario breeds boredom in the students and leads to learning that is quickly forgotten after it is memorized for the required test. Even the best-laid plans that are rich in the Design Qualities can fail in the hands of teachers who still believe they are there to perform for their students.

> Thus the idea that great teachers are also great performers, even actors, is usually well received by many teachers, for acting is so much of what they are required to do. It will always be so, at least until schools are organized around the performances of students rather than the performances of teachers. (Schlechty, 1997, p. 44)

The Collaborative Professional Development Process is organized around the performances of students and what these performances tell us about the teachers who designed and implemented the lessons. For this process to be fully successful, teachers must be willing to honestly examine their roles in the learning process. They must be willing to shift from viewing themselves as the actor—the Sage on Stage—to seeing their role in the classroom as one that is constantly changing and evolving to meet the needs of their students. Educators can at times be facilitators, experts, or even co-learners alongside their students. In these classrooms, the teachers let their students take the center stage, allowing them to become active participants in the learning process. At the same time, these teachers model and encourage independent thinking.

Many quality individual lessons and units of study begin with teachers in the role of experts. It is during this time that the foundation is laid for the content to be covered. During this initial stage of the lesson or unit of study, it is important for the teachers to use their content expertise to hook the students on the topic and challenge them to become involved. However, it is imperative that teachers move on to the role of facilitator or co-learner early on, so that the students become active participants and share the responsibility for their learning experiences. As a facilitator, the teacher's main purpose is to encourage and develop the cognitive processes that strengthen the thinking skills and behaviors of self-directed learners (see Chapter 2). This is accomplished by encouraging the students' questions and making sure that the necessary resources are available to them to ensure success and minimize frustration. At the same time, teachers must attend to the usual classroom tasks of time management and the encouragement of positive, productive behavior. Group dynamics and cooperative team member strategies are also a focus for the facilitator. It is vital for teachers to be open-minded enough to sometimes become co-learners with their students. By becoming part of the students' learning circle, teachers can have a tremendous impact on the thinking skills and behaviors of their students. During this collaboration, the teachers should model the desired thinking skills and behaviors (see Chapter 2) as they assist the students with their inquiry and exploration of the given topics. By doing so, the teachers are encouraging their students to become intellectually engaged in the learning experiences.

Teachers should naturally blend together their roles of expert, facilitator, and co-learner during any given lesson or unit of study. Educators who encourage their students to become actively involved in the learning experience will find that their roles in the classroom are constantly changing. The keys to these changes are the behaviors and needs of their students as they make the shift from being passive spectators to central players in their learning experiences. In classrooms where this is true, the teachers' roles constantly change, creating rich blends of expertise, challenge, support, encouragement, and praise to guide their students' learning. In these classrooms, there is a seamless blend between students as workers and teachers as facilitators, and the students' sense of ownership and pride in their work flourishes.

To help educators recognize and strengthen their varying roles in the classroom, it is suggested that educators keep a daily list of the roles they play in their students' learning processes. A simple checklist (Figure 8.1) will help educators quickly recognize the roles they assume most often and those they need to strengthen. At the same time, it will help educators track how they have made adjustments throughout the implementation of the lesson to meet the needs of their students. It is unrealistic to assume that teachers can do this for every lesson every day. To start, educators should target a different lesson or class each day to document the roles they assume. This checklist can also be used during the educators' analysis and reflective stages of the Collaborative Professional Development Process.

CLASSROOM COMMUNITIES

As I visited schools and interviewed teachers, students, and administrators, definite patterns started to emerge with respect to the types of classroom communities that teachers create for their students. The classrooms could be divided into three distinct categories: teacher directed, teacher planned and facilitated, and student centered. A brief review of these three categories will illustrate the importance of the classroom community and its impact on students' learning.

Teacher-Directed Classrooms

The teacher-directed classrooms were very traditional, with all the desks in neat, tidy rows facing the central blackboard from which the teachers conducted their lessons. The desks were spaced so as to maintain control and prohibit interaction between the students. The focal point of these teacher-centered classrooms was the place where the teachers stood to

Figure 8.1   Checklist of Roles Assumed by the Teacher

Roles the teacher assumed during classroom implementation of lessons:

Class session: _____   Class session: _____

    (Indicate with check)   (Indicate with check)

    Expert: _____   Expert: _____

    Facilitator: _____   Facilitator: _____

    Co-learner: _____   Co-learner: _____

****

Class session: _____   Class session: _____

    (Indicate with check)   (Indicate with check)

    Expert: _____   Expert: _____

    Facilitator: _____   Facilitator: _____

    Co-learner: _____   Co-learner: _____

****

Class session: _____   Class session: _____

    (Indicate with check)   (Indicate with check)

    Expert: _____   Expert: _____

    Facilitator: _____   Facilitator: _____

    Co-learner: _____   Co-learner: _____

deliver their lessons for their passive students to digest. Students were assigned work in the district-adopted textbooks and reminded that they would be tested on the material at a future date. One school in particular was very proud of their "progressive" multi-aged kindergarten/first grade program. At first, it appeared to be very different from the traditional structure because the students did not sit at desks the entire day. They were brought together for large-group instruction and then went to various rooms and teachers for further study. On closer observation, very little was different from what I saw in the teacher-centered traditional setting. When the students were gathered on the rug for large-group instruction, they had assigned spots and were allowed no interaction with each other. When called upon by the teacher during the beginning morning activities, the students had to respond in the correct order and exact wording that the teacher directed. When they went to the various rooms for further study, all the students were doing exactly the same teacher-planned projects, centered on the textbooks the teachers so strictly adhered to.

Teacher-Planned and Facilitated Classrooms

A third-grade classroom I visited will serve as an illustration of the teacher-planned and facilitated classroom. Upon entering this particular classroom, it was easy to see that all the students were "activity" engaged and seemed excited about what they were doing. They were seated in table groupings of four as they studied the four seasons. Each table grouping was set up as a center for writing poetry, writing stories, painting pictures, counting and sorting leaves that they had collected on their recent nature walk, and computer work aided by parent volunteers. As the teacher walked around the room helping various groups of students and talking with the parent volunteers, it appeared to be drastically different from the traditional classroom. The curriculum in this classroom was integrated around a central theme, and the students were encouraged to work together and share their ideas on the various projects. The teacher's role had changed from an actor dispensing knowledge to her audience to a facilitator coordinating the various teacher-planned activities. It would be easy to think this was truly a student-centered room until a closer look was taken. I did just that when I talked to a little blue-eyed girl seated at the poetry writing center.

As I talked to her, the anxiety she was feeling was written all over her little pixie face. She was distressed over the fact that she had to write a poem about nature "because that is what the teacher told her she had to do at that center." She lamented how much easier the assignment would be if she could write about the gold medal she was wearing around her neck. She shared with me how she had won two of the events at the swim meet over the weekend and how badly she wanted to write about this meaningful event in her life. What was the missing link in a classroom like this? Why was this child, even in the midst of all this activity, so unmotivated? Why was she displaying no signs of being allowed or encouraged to be a self-directed learner?

Student-Centered Classrooms

The missing link was found when I visited student-centered classrooms. One classroom was particularly impressive. It was a fourth-grade classroom of about fifty students and two teachers who team-taught. As I entered the classroom about ten minutes before the morning bell was to ring, there was already excitement in the air. The students were starting their work without any direction from the teachers. They were engaged in a variety of different activities as the teachers began individual conferences with several students. The morning announcements from the office were actually a distraction because the learning had already begun in this classroom.

As I moved around the room, I had the opportunity to converse with the students about what had them so engaged. They told me that their unit of study had begun with a study of the plight of the homeless in the United States, and now they were taking a closer look at the homeless in their own city. Some of the students were creating poetry, creative writing, and art work centered on the homeless in their town. Other students were writing letters to area businesses, asking for monetary donations for the local homeless shelter. One small group of girls was planning their drive to collect personal hygiene items for the females who frequented the homeless shelter. A student working alone at one of the computers was calculating how much money the shelter needed to operate for one week with an average of ten people sleeping there and eating one meal there nightly. When I asked the students who had assigned the activities they were working on, they seemed truly surprised. They told me they decided themselves and then the teachers approved the activities. During my morning visit, I watched as the teachers held "minilessons" on how adjectives can make your writing more colorful. They offered encouragement and praise during private conferences with students to discuss their progress on individual goals. The teachers' genuine interest and praise was evident as they helped students add work samples to their portfolios, with descriptions of why each piece of work was chosen to showcase their progress. I witnessed the teachers as co-learners, working alongside students, seeking information along with their students to answer their questions on the topic at hand. The whole classroom was structured on lessons incorporating the Design Qualities (see Chapter 7). The classroom community was student centered and inquiry and exploration were encouraged. There was an atmosphere of cooperation and respect, and interactions between students, and between students and teachers, were nurtured. Intellectual engagement thrived, as evidenced by the higher-level thinking skills and the behaviors that the students were exhibiting. The lesson was obviously built on the Design Qualities, and the Intellectual Engagement Indicators displayed by the students clearly indicated they had been encouraged and nurtured and were truly becoming habits of the students' minds. This rich classroom community supported a powerful learning experience for everyone involved—even those, like myself, only there to observe.

These three categories of classroom communities illustrate the importance of the atmosphere and learning community all teachers have the power to create for their students. Of course, there are many variations on the specific activities and structure of the student-centered classroom that can give the same result. I am not advocating carbon-copied classrooms; however, by discussing these categories I am giving educators a sense of the type of classroom community that is conducive to the success of quality lessons. Lessons that are designed to encourage intellectual engagement of the students. Lessons where the thinking skills that promote self-directed learning are encouraged, modeled, and practiced until they are so ingrained in the students that they become habits, and self-directed learning thrives.

In conclusion, the successful implementation of quality lessons involves many elements. Teachers must monitor the roles they are assuming, ensure that their classroom communities are student centered, and make adjustments when necessary. At the same time, teachers must analyze whether the desired Design Qualities and Intellectual Engagement Indicators are evident in the classroom. These are all vital parts of the implementation and analysis process that leads to the creation of highly productive collaborative classrooms. In these classrooms, the students and teachers strive for the common goal of empowering the students to become self-directed, lifelong learners.

9

Analyzing Lessons as They Unfold

How can educators tell whether or not their use of the Collaborative Professional Development Process is creating the results they want in their classrooms? They know they are planning lessons with the Design Qualities in mind. They have a sense that they are seeing more intellectual engagement with the students. They want some confirmation that they are on the right track, but the next Guided Collaborative Discussion of Student Work is scheduled for several weeks in the future. What can they do to ensure that this venture is working? They need not wait for a month of lessons to go by before they determine the effectiveness of this professional venture. The observations they make in the classroom will provide opportunities to analyze whether the results are indeed what they had anticipated. They need to be able to think on their feet as the lessons unfold under their directions. Remember that they designed the work for their students. It is up to them to monitor the effectiveness of the lessons in their classrooms.

At the beginning of the Collaborative Professional Development Process, when educators complete the Personal Teaching Inventory (see Chapter 4), many find the "An Educator's Practice in the Presence of Students" section is an area needing attention. These same teachers might excel at planning units and lessons, but making these "paper lessons" come alive with the students is another challenge altogether. Teachers who master unit planning need to stay true to their well-designed plans, yet not ignore the fact that they must monitor the plans' effectiveness during the lessons with the students. So what should be done?

STAYING TRUE TO LESSON DESIGN

Once teachers have designed quality lessons using the Design Qualities (see Chapter 7), the next step is staying true to the lesson design during implementation. This does not mean being inflexible during the implementation. All quality teachers know that adjustments need to be made to meet the ever-changing needs of their students. At the same time, it is important to seize upon the unforeseen situations that give teachers the opportunity to create a unique, unplanned teachable moment. Staying true to lesson design means making sure that during implementation the Design Qualities embedded in the lessons result in the intellectual engagement of the students. The indicator of this intellectual engagement is the students' acquisition of the content knowledge through the observable use of higher-level thinking skills and behaviors. These are the skills and behaviors that in themselves promote self-directed learning.

It is understood that teachers will be familiar with the lessons prior to walking into the classroom. They should be aware of the Design Qualities they incorporated into the lessons. They should be able to picture what will occur as the lessons progress, and they should be able to visualize the anticipated student intellectual engagement. For example, consider the lessons described below.

Example 1: Listen to the Students

The educator selected the Design Quality "Novelty and Variety" as the emphasis for a lesson that requires students to present the information they compiled during research for a social studies class. He pictured the students displaying evidence of the Intellectual Engagement Indicator "Using All the Senses." He instructed the students to select from a great variety of products to demonstrate their findings. He anticipated small dramas, works of art, lyrics to songs, research papers, board games, and so on. But during in-class time provided for the initial planning of the students' projects, he observes that most of the students are planning to produce two-page reports.

Although it might be surprising that the students are taking such a traditional approach, this is an opportunity for the educator to monitor and address the situation. The educator's on-the-spot analysis is vital if he wants to persevere with this well-designed lesson. He needs to consider what caused this situation. As the teacher, he might need to ponder whether some other method of communicating with the students was speaking louder than his words. Was his plan to incorporate "Novelty and Variety" a sincere effort? Was there greater emphasis placed on one idea over another? Did it seem that he valued one form of presentation over another? He needs to talk to the students. He needs to listen to the reasons they give for selecting the traditional course of action. Are they more comfortable with the predictability of grades given on written projects? Are they worried that selecting a new format would cause their projects to be judged differently? Did they truly understand their options? Listening to the students is one way for an educator to adjust on the spot. Once he has heard the comments of his students, it is time to adjust. He might need to consider developing rubrics with the students that demonstrate the methods of evaluation of their projects. He might tell them directly that he was trying to encourage greater novelty and variety in their presentations. Witnessing his students' original reluctance to attempt new approaches, and knowing that he needed to address this, is analysis in action. Resolving situations like this together elevates everyone's interaction and intellectual engagement in the classroom.

Example 2: Meet the Needs of the Students

The educator selected the Design Quality "Choice" to be the emphasis of the lesson. The students are to conduct an Internet search for the differences in childcare in various cultures. This will culminate in a class discussion on work and family. The educator anticipates that the students will find a great variety of sources and will display the Indicator of Intellectual Engagement "Wonderment, Inquisitiveness, Curiosity, and the Enjoyment of Problem Solving" as they consider the different roles and routines of various cultures. However, as the educator wanders from student to student in the computer lab, she notices that most of the students are eventually sharing the same Internet site and not locating varied references as she had anticipated.

As this lesson unfolds, once again the educator must analyze on the spot to adjust the situation. Maybe this time the students are unable to explain convincingly why one site appeals to them over the others. As the educator asks students to select passages to quote from alternative sites, it becomes clear that many of the other sites have a vocabulary that is beyond the reading level of the majority of the students in her class. Ultimately, she needs to adjust the number of sources the students are required to cite, and she may decide in the future to select predetermined sites for the students until they master more effective research techniques. This "thinking on her feet" is the analysis stage of the Collaborative Professional Development Process that is so vital to successful implementation of lessons.

USING QUICK REFERENCE CHARTS

In order to make analysis during lesson implementation a more likely occurrence, in the beginning teachers should use the quick reference charts (Figures 9.1 and 9.2) to help them track the embedded Design Qualities and the resulting Intellectual Engagement Indicators that they are promoting in the lesson. A simple check mark on the charts will indicate that the Design Qualities and the intellectual engagement of the students were

Figure 9.1   Design Qualities Quick Reference Chart

Design Qualities	Anticipated	Witnessed	Adjusted
Product Focus			
Clear and Compelling Product Standards			
Protection From Adverse Consequences			
Affirmation of Performance			
Affiliation			
Novelty and Variety			
Choice			
Authenticity			
Organization of Knowledge			
Content and Substance			

Figure 9.2   Intellectual Engagement Indicators Quick Reference Chart

Intellectual Engagement Indicators	Anticipated	Witnessed	Adjusted
Persistence			
Listening to Others With Understanding and Empathy			
Striving for Accuracy and Precision			
Decreasing Impulsivity			
Cooperative Thinking			
Reflection			
Using All the Senses			
Displaying a Sense of Humor			
Questioning and Problem Posing			
Drawing on Past Knowledge and Applying It to New Situations			
Ingenuity, Originality, Insight, Creativity			
Risk Taking			
Wonderment, Inquisitiveness, Curiosity, and the Enjoyment of Problem Solving			
Metacognition			

planned and then observed in the classroom. Throughout the lesson, the teacher can make adjustments as needed if the intended elements of the lesson are not developing. This adjustment can also be noted with a check mark on the charts. Adjusting their roles and emphasizing the designated Design Qualities can help teachers steer the learning experience to promote the intended intellectual engagement. After time, teachers will become so adept at recognizing these indicators and making adjustments to ensure them, it will no longer be necessary to use the charts. However, in the beginning many educators find them to be helpful reminders during instruction. The quick reference charts can also be used during Collaborative Discussion of Student Work and the subsequent development of the Professional Development Plan.

OBSERVATION BY TRUSTED COLLEAGUES

Another way that educators can perfect their abilities to analyze during lesson implementation, and at the same time receive immediate feedback, is to arrange for classroom visits by trusted colleagues. Since the Guided Collaborative Discussion of Student Work is conducted with a group of trusted colleagues already, these same people could visit each other's classrooms to give suggestions on how to perfect the art of analyzing and making adjustments during instruction to improve the intellectual engagement of the students. These observations could be regulated by guidelines that the colleagues develop together, to help keep the focus of the observations on track. Regular discussions with trusted peers can help educators analyze and make adjustments to ensure constant progress.

If visits are difficult to arrange, or educators are just not comfortable with classroom visits, another way educators can take a step back and look more analytically at their practices is to videotape lessons. Afterwards, they can examine the videotapes for evidence they anticipated when they designed the lessons. This is also an ideal way for educators to see how they handle making adjustments on the spot when things are not going as they planned. The videotapes could be viewed alone or with trusted colleagues.

CLASSROOM DISCUSSION

Regardless of the methods educators use to improve their abilities to analyze and make adjustments in their classrooms, a brief discussion with their students at the end of the lesson is always a good way to add depth to their practices. Having the students discuss the intellectual skills and behaviors they used during the lessons will help the teachers and the students recognize evidence of these skills and behaviors in the learning environments and the way the teachers' abilities to analyze and intervene orchestrated and supported them. At the same time, it will give the students concrete examples of how these process skills and behaviors look and feel, and how they can help the students achieve their personal learning goals in the classroom.

REFLECTION

It is very important for teachers to document the analyses and interventions they make in order to improve this part of their practices. Including this documentation in their daily reflective journals will help educators reflect on the progress they are making and at the same time help them to develop strategies for improvement. These journal entries are vital pieces of evidence that every educator should refer to during the development of his or her Professional Development Plan.

There has been a strong emphasis placed on reflection in this Collaborative Professional Development Process, but the time to do in-depth reflection is after the lesson is completed. Letting an entire lesson go by without analyzing it on the spot is an opportunity lost and a negation of the time and talent spent on developing a sound lesson in the first place.

PULLING IT ALL TOGETHER

This book began by stating the questions that many educators ask themselves when faced with a new educational initiative:

- "Will this make me a better educator?"
- "Will this have an impact on my entire practice?"
- "Will this enhance my students' learning?"
- "Will this simplify my life?"

Educators who are using the Collaborative Professional Development Process to direct their professional endeavors in and out of their classrooms answer all these questions with a resounding "Yes." Dramatic changes occur in the intellectual engagement of students when teachers take the initiative to open their classroom doors, collaborate with their fellow educators, and elevate their professional practices. The teacher's practices are worthy of praise—not because of the teacher's behavior, but because of the evidence of high student intellectual engagement and achievement.

I know what it is like for the average educator to try to find the time to take on one more new endeavor. That is why I designed the Collaborative Professional Development Process to be incorporated into the many tasks educators are already performing daily. Truly committed educators are not afraid of taking on a challenge when they know their students' success depends on their constantly trying to better themselves as educators.

Today, quality educators are holding their students to higher and higher standards—standards that are demanded by institutes of higher education as well as the labor market. So why not hold yourself to these higher standards as well? This is an opportunity for educators to fine tune their practices and bring about results that will be visible to everyone who enters their classrooms.

To make this endeavor run as smoothly as possible, I have provided a school calendar with each step of the Collaborative Professional Development Process scheduled (see Resource on pages 115 to 120). Although the process could be initiated at any time in the school year, starting in September (or the first month of the school calendar) is ideal because it will allow enough time to incorporate the process at a comfortable pace, given the demands of an average school year.

Every component of the Collaborative Professional Development Process is designed to strengthen educators' practices. For some, it may not be feasible to implement the entire process during one school year. Many educators prefer to concentrate on a few Design Qualities or Intellectual Engagement Indicators at a time, instead of working with all of them right from the start. In that case, implementing the process over a two-year period would be the answer. Others may find certain components, such as the Guided Collaborative Discussion of Student Work, so powerful that they can incorporate only that part of the process into their practices immediately. Teachers need to find their comfort zones and start with the components that they feel their practices are ready to handle.

Teachers everywhere are busy, but the time invested in the Collaborative Professional Development Process will affect every aspect of an educator's professional practice. With the Collaborative Professional Development Process, educators will empower themselves and their students to become lifelong learners. Their lives will become exciting adventures in which intellectual engagement will thrive. These memorable teachers will not only touch their students' lives, but will also equip their students to elevate their "dances of life" to stages far beyond their imaginations.

Resource

School Calendar of Collaborative Professional Development Activities

In the school calendar following, each step of the Collaborative Professional Development Process is scheduled so that the collaborative learning teams can complete the process at a comfortable pace, given the demands of an average school year. The dates of meetings and deadlines will be noted in the blank Monday through Friday blocks. All members of the collaborative learning teams should keep their own copies of the calendar for quick reference throughout the school year.

SEPTEMBER

Week	Item	Monday	Tuesday	Wednesday	Thursday	Friday
1	Begin daily reflective journal					
2	Choose collaborative learning team members					
3	Team's first meeting, to establish common understandings					
4	Team's second meeting, to establish common understandings Teachers complete Personal Teaching Inventories					

OCTOBER

Week	Item	Monday	Tuesday	Wednesday	Thursday	Friday
1	Team meets to continue common understandings study					
	Team sets meeting dates for the remainder of the school year					
2						
3	Educators set up their Professional Development Portfolios					
4	First Guided Collaborative Discussion of Student Work session					

NOVEMBER

Week	Item	Monday	Tuesday	Wednesday	Thursday	Friday
1	Educators begin to develop Professional Development Plans					
2	Second Guided Collaborative Discussion of Student Work session					
3	Educators identify "focus" for their Professional Development Plans					
4	Educators begin to work on their professional development goals					

DECEMBER

Week	Item	Monday	Tuesday	Wednesday	Thursday	Friday
1	Third Guided Collaborative Discussion of Student Work session					
2	Continued work on Professional Development Focus					
3	Happy Holidays!					
4	Happy Holidays!					

JANUARY

This is a good month to hold two discussions of student work sessions, if possible

Week	Item	Monday	Tuesday	Wednesday	Thursday	Friday
1						
2	Fourth Guided Collaborative Discussion of Student Work session					
3						
4	Fifth Guided Collaborative Discussion of Student Work session					

FEBRUARY

Week	Item	Monday	Tuesday	Wednesday	Thursday	Friday
1	Make sure to continue daily reflective journals					
2						
3	Sixth Guided Collaborative Discussion of Student Work session					
4						

MARCH

Week	Item	Monday	Tuesday	Wednesday	Thursday	Friday
1	Seventh Guided Collaborative Discussion of Student Work session					
2	Continue to refine and strengthen Professional Development Plans					
3						
4	Have fun on Spring Break!					

APRIL

Here's another good month to hold two discussions of student work sessions, if possible

Week	Item	Monday	Tuesday	Wednesday	Thursday	Friday
1						
2	Eighth Guided Collaborative Discussion of Student Work session					
3						
4	Ninth Guided Collaborative Discussion of Student Work session					

MAY

Week	Item	Monday	Tuesday	Wednesday	Thursday	Friday
1	Tenth Guided Collaborative Discussion of Student Work session					
2	Hold a workshop to share the Collaborative Professional Development Process with colleagues who are not on a collaborative team this year					
3	All who are willing share their Professional Development Portfolios					
4						

JUNE

Week	Item	Monday	Tuesday	Wednesday	Thursday	Friday
1	Squeeze in one last Guided Collaborative Discussion of Student Work session, if possible					
2	Continue to research and strengthen Professional Practices over the summer					
3						
4	Enjoy a well-deserved rest!					

Bibliography

Allen, D. (Ed.). (1998). *Assessing student learning: From grading to understanding.* New York: Teachers College Press.

Block, P. (1996). *Enhancing professional practice: A framework for teaching.* San Francisco: Berret-Koehler.

Blythe, T., Allen, D., & Powell, B. (1999). *Looking together at student work.* New York: Teachers College Press.

California Standards for the Teaching Profession. (1997). Retrieved September, 1999, from www.btsa.ca.gov/ba/pubs/pdf/cstpreport.pdf

Center for Leadership in School Reform. (2003). Retrieved January, 2003, from www.clsr.org

Coalition of Essential Schools Nationalweb. (2002). Retrieved April, 2002, from www.essentialschools.org

The Collaborative Assessment Conference. (n.d.). Retrieved September, 2002, from www.lasw.org/CAC_description.html

Costa, A. L. (2001). *Developing minds: Programs for teaching thinking* (3rd ed.). Alexandria, VA: Association for Supervision and Curriculum Development.

Costa, A., & Garmston, R. (2002). *Cognitive coaching: A foundation for renaissance schools* (2nd ed.). Norwood, MA: Christopher-Gordon.

Costa, A., & Kallick, B. (2000). *Habits of mind: A developmental series.* Alexandria, VA: Association for Supervision and Curriculum Development.

Costa, A., & Liebmann, R. M. (Eds.). (1997a). *Envisioning process as content: Toward a renaissance curriculum.* Thousand Oaks, CA: Corwin Press.

Costa, A., & Liebmann, R. M. (1997b). *The process-centered school: Sustaining a renaissance community.* Thousand Oaks, CA: Corwin Press.

Costa, A., & Liebmann, R. M. (1997c). *Supporting the spirit of learning: When process is content.* Thousand Oaks, CA: Corwin Press.

Costa, A. L., & Lowery, L. F. (1991). *Techniques for teaching thinking.* Pacific Grove, CA: Critical Thinking Press.

Cushman, K. (1996, November). Looking collaboratively at student work: An essential toolkit. *Horace, 13*(2).

Cushman, K. (1999, April). The cycle of inquiry and action: Essential learning communities. *Horace, 15*(4).

Danielson, C. (1966). *Enhancing professional practice: A framework for teaching.* Alexandria, VA: Association for Supervision and Curriculum Development.

Darling-Hammond, L., Ancess, J., & Falk, B. (1995). *Authentic assessment in action: Studies of schools and students at work.* New York: Teachers College Press.

Dewey, J. (1933). *How we think.* Boston: D. C. Heath.

Dunne, D. W. (2000). *Teachers learn from looking together at student work.* Retrieved November, 2002, from www.education-world.com

Eby, J. W., & Kujawa, E. (1994). *Reflective planning, teaching and evaluation: K–12.* New York: Macmillan.

The Education Trust. (1995). *Standards in practice.* Washington, DC: Author.

Featherstone, H. (Ed.). (1998, Spring).Teachers looking closely at students and their work. *Changing Minds*, Bulletin 13.

Graham, B., & Fahey, K. (1999, March). School leaders look at student work. *Educational Leadership, 56*(6), 25-27.

Grant, G., & Murray, C. (1999). *Teaching in America: The slow revolution.* Cambridge: Harvard University Press.

Habits of Mind. Retrieved January, 2002, from www.habits-of-mind.net

Herald-Taylor, B. G. (1966, March). Three paradigms for literature instruction in grades 3–6. *Reading Teacher, 49*, 456-466.

Hirsh, S. (2002, October). Together, you can do more. *Results Newsletter.* Retrieved December, 2002, from www.nsdc.org/educatorindex.htm

Howey, K., & Zimpher, N. (1988, May). *University contributions: Designing a peer assistance and review program.* Columbus: The Ohio State University.

Huff, D. (2000, November). Teachers examining student work to guide curriculum, instruction. *Education Week.* Retrieved February, 2001, from www.edweek.org

Kelly, T. F. (1999, March). Why state mandates don't work. *Phi Delta Kappan, 80*(7), 543-544, 546.

Lasley, T. J. (1992). Promoting teacher reflection. *Journal of Staff Development, 13*(1), 24-29.

Lieberman, A., & Miller, L. (2001). *Teachers caught in the action: Professional development that matters.* New York: Teachers College Press.

Looking at student work. (n.d.). Retrieved April, 2002, from www.lasw.org

Mann, L. (1999, March). New Goals for Teacher Evaluation. *ASCD Education Update, 41*, 1-8.

Manning, M., & Manning, G. (1993, May). Remarkable researchers in first grade. *Teaching K-8*, 54-56.

Martin, P., & Haselkorn, S. (1998, November). *Boston plan for excellence: Teaching does make a difference and students can meet the standards.* Washington, DC: The Education Trust.

McTighe, J. (1994, September). *Developing performance assessment tasks: Template for designers.* Frederick, MD: Maryland Assessment Consortium.

National Board for Professional Teaching Standards. (n.d.). *Standards.* Retrieved September, 1999, from www.nbpts.org/standards/stdsoverviews.cfm

National Board for Professional Teaching Standards. (1991). *Toward high and rigorous standards.* Detroit, MI: Author.

National Staff Development Council. (2001). *Standards for Staff Development.* Retrieved October, 2002, from www.nsdc.org/educatorindex.htm

Newmann, F. M., & Wehlage, G. C. (1993, April). Five standards of authentic instruction. *Educational Leadership, 50*(7), 8-12.

Peer Assistance and Review: Working Models Across the Country. (2000). Retrieved May, 2000, from www.calstate.edu/ier/reports/PARReport.pdf

PRAXIS III: Classroom Performance Assessment for Beginning Teachers. (1992). Retrieved September, 1999, from www.bgsu.edu/colleges/edhd/programs/MentorNet/pathprax.html

Pugach, M. C., & Johnson, L. J. (1990). Developing reflective practice through structured dialogue. In R. T. Clift, W. R. Houseon, & M. C. Pugach (Eds.), *Encouraging reflective practice in education: An analysis of issues and programs* (pp. 186-201). New York: Teachers College Press.

Rallis, S. & Zajano, N. (1997, May). Keeping the faith until the outcomes are obvious. *Phi Delta Kappan, 78*(9), 706–709.

Richardson, J. (2001, February). Student work at the core of teacher learning. *Results Newsletter.* Retrieved June, 2001, from www.nsdc.org/educatorindex.htm

Schlechty, P. C. (1997). *Inventing better schools. An action plan for educational reform.* San Francisco: Jossey-Bass.

Schlechty, P. C. (1999, January). *Tools for building capacity.* Louisville, KY: Center for Leadership in School Reform.

Schnitzer, S. (1993, April). Designing an authentic assessment. *Educational Leadership, 50*(9), 32–35.

Schon, D. A. (1983). *The reflective practitioner: How professionals think in action.* New York: Basic Books.

Schon, D. A. (1990, February). *Educating the reflective practitioner: Toward a new design for teaching and learning in the professions.* San Francisco: Jossey-Bass.

Stepien, W., & Gallagher, S. (1993, April). Problem-based learning: As authentic as it gets. *Educational Leadership, 50*(7), 25-28.

Taggart, G. L., & Wilson, A. P. (1998). *Promoting reflective thinking in teachers: 44 action strategies.* Thousand Oaks, CA: Corwin Press.

Traver, R. (1998, March). What is a good guiding question? *Educational Leadership,* 70–73.

The Tuning Protocol. (n.d.). Retrieved September, 2002, from www.lasw.org/Tuning_description.html

U.S. National Research Center. (1999). *Third International Mathematics and Science Study: Summary of Findings.* Retrieved January, 2000, from ustimss.msu.edu

Wassermann, S. (1999, February). Shazam! You're a teacher: Facing the illusory quest for certainty in classroom practice. *Phi Delta Kappan, 80*(6), 464-468.

Wasserstein, P. (1995, September). What middle schoolers say about their school-work. *Educational Leadership, 53,* 41–43.

Wiggins, G., & McTighe, J. (1998). *Understanding by design.* Alexandria, VA: Association for Supervision and Curriculum Development.

Wong, H. K., & Wong, R. T. (1998). *The first days of school.* Mountain View, CA: Harry Wong Publications.

Index

Page references followed by *fig* indicate an illustrated figure.